D1477359

First published in Great Britain in 2018 by

Policy Press
University of Bristol
1-9 Old Park Hill
Bristol
BS2 8BB
UK
t: +44 (0)117 954 5940
pp-info@bristol.ac.uk
www.policypress.co.uk

North America office:
Policy Press
c/o The University of Chicago Press
1427 East 60th Street
Chicago, IL 60637, USA
t: +1 773 702 7700
f: +1 773 702 9756
sales@press.uchicago.edu
www.press.uchicago.edu

British Library Cataloguing in Publication Data
A catalogue record for this book is available from the British Library.

Library of Congress Cataloging-in-Publication Data
A catalog record for this book has been requested.

ISBN 978-1-4473-4447-6 (hardback)
ISBN 978-1-4473-4448-3 (ePub)
ISBN 978-1-4473-4449-0 (Mobi)
ISBN 978-1-4473-4450-6 (OA PDF)

Cover design by Policy Press
Front cover: image kindly supplied by Sam Church
Printed and bound in Great Britain by CPI Group (UK) Ltd,
Croydon, CR0 4YY
Policy Press uses environmentally responsible print partners

Contents

Acknowledgements

Every book is a team effort. Any advancement of scholarship can be attributed to the synergy from collaborative relationships. I am grateful to my colleagues in the University of Bristol Law School and in the Bristol Institute for Migration and Mobility Studies, especially Chris Bertram, Jon Fox, Tonia Novitz, Tony Prosser and Ann Singleton, who supported me during the research and writing process with their comments and encouragement. Heartfelt thanks go to Robert Eyles, who researched various aspects of British citizenship and belonging in 2017, commented on each draft chapter, and brought his own intellectual spark to this work.

The Economic and Social Research Council (ESRC) provided a grant (ES/L010356/1) for research on British citizenship. The University of Bristol Law School supported the research with departmental funding and research time over 2016-17. In 2016-17, I taught students in the University of Bristol Law School an optional unit on British citizenship, which I designed from the findings of my ESRC project on British citizenship. This was a productive intellectual period during which I discussed my research daily with a set of engaged students. PolicyBristol funded a storytelling event in Bristol in 2016. Various interviewees gave me their valuable time for no tangible gain to themselves but for the opportunity to tell their stories. Conferences in Mexico City (2017 Law and Society Association International Meeting) and in Newcastle, UK (2017 Socio-Legal Studies Association Meeting) were wonderful forums for gaining ideas and feedback. Three anonymous reviewers rigorously reviewed the book and provided thoughtful comments, which helped deepen my work.

Finally, it has been a pleasure to work with some fantastic professionals during the production of this book: Victoria Pittman, Senior Editor at Policy Press/Bristol University Press, Shannon Kneis, Editorial Assistant at Policy Press/Bristol University Press, Ruth Wallace, Production Editor at Policy Press/Bristol University Press, Kathryn King, Marketing Manager at Policy Press/Bristol University Press and Phylicia Ulibarri-Eglite, Marketing Coordinator at Policy Press/Bristol University Press, who have provided guidance whenever required; artist Sam Church, whose beautiful illustrations adorn the book; and Marie Selwood, who has meticulously proofread the manuscript and prepared the index to this book.

Preface

Britishness, belonging and citizenship: Experiencing nationality law is a book about the lives of migrants who become British citizens (termed migrant–citizens for ease of reference in this book) drawn from their life stories. What do their experiences reveal about the links between citizenship and belonging? How does the process of applying for British citizenship affect those who make applications? How can the experience be improved for future applicants for British citizenship? Seeking to connect the sociological with the legal, the book presents some urgent considerations for reform.

Most migrant–citizens migrated as strangers to this land and then resided for a long period of time to become British citizens. They exemplify 'the stranger' idealised by prolific sociological and philosophical thinker Georg Simmel (1971) in his eponymous essay. Simmel (1971, p 143) writes about the resident stranger as 'not ... the wanderer who comes today and goes tomorrow, but rather as the person who comes today and stays tomorrow'. These strangers are relative newcomers to the land but are not transient visitors. They are successful in entering legally and fulfilling all requirements for acquiring citizenship over time.

This book is a quest for untold stories. With the exception of research on citizenship ceremonies (for example, Byrne, 2014), there is little on record about the experiences of citizenship processes and the meaning of citizenship for those who successfully undertake the journey. Lawyers generally lose contact with successful applicants. This book originated in multiple conversations with practitioners who did not know how citizenship applicant clients subsequently fared in life. Lawyers had more contact with failed applicants who had further need for legal assistance. One lawyer spoke of how, after assisting a client for nearly 10 years in the immigration and citizenship legal process, she was pained when he did not stay in touch.

The citizenship process becomes a personal memory for successful applicants, but institutional memory is lost as when the citizenship application process is over, the successful applicants just carry on with their lives: education, families, jobs, leisure and travel. Their stories remain undocumented. Gathering and analysing this elusive data, the book investigates what citizenship means to applicants who successfully undergo the application process for British citizenship. It highlights the processes of inclusion and exclusion that are experienced by long-term residents (the 'politics of belonging').

It seems particularly important to tap into the experiences of past applicants of British citizenship because of the current uncertainty of legal status for more than three million long-term UK-resident nationals from the European Economic Area (EAA). Many EEA nationals have been present in the UK for years without seeking formal citizenship because, as EEA nationals, they were treated nearly the same as citizens for purposes such as entry, seeking employment and education, travel, bringing in family members and continuous residence. Now, as the UK prepares to withdraw from the European Union (EU) – a process known as 'Brexit' – they are unsure of what the future holds for them. Depending on their personal circumstances and choices, the EEA nationals in the UK may or may not decide to opt for British citizenship. Contradictory trends are observable on naturalisation in contemporary Britain. While there is a rush of citizenship and permanent residence applications in the UK from some EEA nationals, there is a contrasting reaction from many others who are reluctant to become British at a time when, should they choose to do so, they may potentially lose EU nationality after Brexit.

The situation of EEA nationals may appear exceptional, but viewing their plight through the long lens of time, we can find many others who have been similarly placed in a precarious position. For instance, in the past there were categories of British protected persons, or people of British lineage with special claims to Britishness, or people from former colonies, who could also claim membership in British society, but who lost their legal protections because of changing geopolitics and personal circumstances that reshaped their situations. Some of them fought legal battles and successfully made their entry into UK, while others are still struggling for their place in British society. These stories are relevant for our contemporary times when long-term resident EEA nationals are being affected by Brexit negotiations so that past mistakes are not repeated.

Stories have special functions in research as they bring in beliefs and emotions to the understanding of belonging and citizenship in a manner that reported legal cases are seldom able to achieve. Stories also provide direct 'user feedback' on naturalisation processes. Using such feedback, recommendations will be made in the concluding chapter so that the process for future applicants can be made more fair and transparent while retaining the features past applicants have found useful. Throughout the intention is to allow the voice of applicants to come through without academic ventriloquism. However, some academic intervention is inevitable while identifying recurrent themes and connecting these to past research and available literature on citizenship.

Several patterns and common themes emerge from the collected experiences of the storytellers. Even though citizenship pathways of people are highly individualistic and varied in nature, for most people the length of time in residence in the country is the single most important factor that generates feelings of belonging. Similarly, a recurring thread is that of the experience of making an application for British citizenship being a bureaucratic one with all the attendant problems such as delays, expenses and anxiety about procedures and outcomes. These appear to chip away at feelings of belonging to the UK. The data indicates that, despite the divergent origins or pathways of people, there is much in common in their citizenship experiences that can be usefully scrutinised. In the inspiring words of the slain MP Jo Cox: 'We are far more united and have far more in common with each other than that which divides us.'[1] Her words reflect a foundational claim of universal human rights and also resonate with the findings of this book on the citizenship experiences of many different people who successfully become British.

ONE

Introduction to trends and concepts in British citizenship

In his poem 'Remember the ship'[2] British-Afro-Guyanese playwright, poet and children's writer John Agard asks everyone to connect the 'ship' and the 'citizen' in 'citizenship'. The metaphor of ship stands for migration, which Agard treats as a foil for understanding citizenship. An apparent connection between citizenship and migration is that new citizens who register or naturalise are generally migrants who have travelled from elsewhere. *Britishness, belonging and citizenship: Experiencing nationality law* explores people's perceptions of British citizenship and the process of applying for citizenship. It lays out the connections between citizenship and its meaning, perceptions of belonging, the politics of belonging, and the effects of applying for citizenship on applicants who become British. Prior to entering the substantive debates and exploring the personal accounts, this chapter addresses some salient features of British citizenship and nationality by way of setting the scene. It presents some broad-brush sketches of developments in British citizenship at the macro-political level so that the individual accounts can be calibrated against these developments and understood in their context.

The origins of citizenship and naturalisation in the UK are murky and subsequent legal developments have been largely ad hoc in nature. Yet, the genesis and genealogy of British citizenship have had lasting effects on the present-day provisions of nationality law, thereby affecting the manner in which people experience contemporary citizenship acquisition processes. An important first step towards understanding the citizenship application experience is to undertake a survey of the origins and dissect the conceptual content of citizenship.

Citizenship: key concepts

Sometimes the word 'citizenship' is used in the general sense of good civic behaviour (for example, corporate citizenship, citizenship in the classroom or even citizenship training for dogs[3]), but when membership in a nation state is at stake, citizenship has a different legal and sociological connotation. When employed in a narrow sense in law, citizenship is a formal, legal status to which some special

legal rights and obligations attach. In a broader sense, citizenship can include identity as well as territorial and group membership. To most storytellers in this book, citizenship is about their legal status as well as associated emotions of belonging. Analysis of the stories also picks up on themes of inclusion and exclusion experienced by people.

A good starting point of analysis for national citizenship is T. H. Marshall's influential 1950 essay on citizenship and social class in Britain. In this essay, Marshall identified three dimensions of citizenship – civil, political and social. He claimed that these three had developed sequentially over the past three centuries, each having led to the other. The civil aspect is exemplified in liberty of person and basic freedoms such as thought, speech and faith. The political aspect can be seen in greater inclusion in voting, eventually leading to universal suffrage. The social aspect of citizenship is about welfare and social security. This claim of sequential progression of rights is, however, now contested by scholars and numerous empirical departures from this sequence have been identified (for example, Turner 2001). Further, Marshall's focus on the individual worker–citizen has been criticised as not being inclusive enough of the contributions of women (who did not always fit in the model of paid worker in the economy). Yet, this essay continues to be relevant as it was the first sociological critique of its kind of the various dimensions of British citizenship. It looked at what kind of state apparatus was required for supporting meaningful citizenship and identified this as a liberal welfare state that could guarantee social rights, as well as civil and political rights.

To what extent is this view supported by law? In case law, the importance of contemporary British citizenship has been set out in clear language in *R v Secretary of State for Home Department Ex Parte Mohammed Fayed* [1996] EWCA Civ 946 (13 November 1996), in which the court examined the refusals of the naturalisation applications of two brothers, both born in Egypt. The brothers (erstwhile owners of the well-known London store Harrods) were refused naturalisation but not informed why they had been refused. The court decided that the brothers needed to be given reasons because citizenship was a valuable asset for them. The brothers had suffered loss when they had been refused citizenship. The court explained, in para 773 e-f:

> Apart from the damaging effect on their reputation of having their application refused the refusal has deprived them of the benefits of citizenship. The benefits are substantial. Besides the intangible benefit of being a citizen of a country which is their and their families' home, there are the tangible benefits which include freedom from immigration control, citizenship of the European Union and the rights which accompany that citizenship, the right to vote and the right to stand in Parliamentary elections.

Through these observations the case reconfirms the Marshallian ingredients of citizenship: civil, political and social as well as economic components. Undoubtedly, other elements also matter. Delanty (2007) discusses how new ideas of citizenship diverge from the Marshallian mould in his work on disciplinary citizenship versus cultural citizenship. He writes that the modern citizen is not just understood from a formal status in the liberal notion or from a consumerist perspective. Rather than merely an emphasis on rights there is a focus on duties and engagement in civil society. Citizenship can also be about cultural content such as through learning and development.

Citizenship: some controversies

Given that citizenship clearly confers benefits on citizenship holders, why is it often controversial? Citizenship has a Janus-faced function of simultaneous inclusion and exclusion. Not all those who present themselves as applicants for membership are perceived to be desirable members. Citizenship acts as a sorting process for 'deserving' candidates. In practice, unless well-established criteria are used, nationality procedures may be capricious and unfair in effect for applicants.

In recent times, citizenship has become a continuation of immigration control with some people excluded from it for economic, social or national security reasons. People can even lose citizenship for reasons of conduct. It is not just at borders where people may be excluded; there can be denial of political rights and personal security within national territory, as well as because of discretion in other types of decisions on inclusion and exclusion from citizenship. Ajit Bhalla and Frédéric Lapeyre (1997, p 420) argue that political exclusion needs to be understood from the notion of the state as representative of society's dominant classes. This means that there is a link between class positions and the withholding of full citizenship status and citizenship rights from certain social groups. In applications by economic migrants and their dependents, this can be observed quite plainly because high fees and requirements for higher educational qualifications and evidence of employment mean that poorer migrants do not have the opportunity to gain permanent status. Rogers Brubaker writes: 'Although citizenship is internally inclusive, it is externally exclusive. There is a conceptually clear, legally consequential, and ideologically charged distinction between citizens and foreigners' (1992, p 21). This also raises difficult questions about how citizenship fits within the human rights framework, which is universally inclusive of all human beings. The United Nations (UN) Universal Declaration of Human Rights is expressly premised on 'the inherent dignity and ... the equal and inalienable rights of all members of the human family'. This extends rights to non-nationals and nationals alike. The Declaration on the Human Rights of Individuals who are not nationals of the country in which they live, adopted by the UN General Assembly in 1985, is emphatic in guaranteeing most civil and political rights to non-nationals. There are limitations on political participation by non-citizens, but apart from these non-nationals cannot be denied basic civil and political rights.

While immigration status and acquisition or loss of nationality lie at the discretion of each individual state, international law can influence the national framing of citizenship. The universal human rights principles operate as limitations on exclusions from national citizenship. Principles of equality and non-discrimination are often pitted against claims of national sovereignty. Statelessness is an area where international law intervenes. Article 15 of the Universal Declaration of Human Rights asserts that everyone has a right to nationality. It is forbidden under international law to leave a person, because of an action by a state, without any nationality, as this results in statelessness. The Convention relating to the Status of Stateless Persons 1954 (Statelessness Convention 1954) was drafted in order to guarantee the protection of these individuals' fundamental rights. Article 1(1) of the Statelessness Convention 1954 defines a stateless person as 'a person who is not recognized as a national by any State under operation of its law'.

Similarly, various children's rights issues are well protected by international law. Article 7 of the Convention on the Rights of the Child states that every child has the right to acquire a nationality, while Article 5 of the Convention on the Elimination of all Forms of Racial Discrimination requires states to 'prohibit and to eliminate racial discrimination in all its forms and to guarantee the right of everyone, without distinction as to race, colour, or national or ethnic origin, to equality before the law, notably in the enjoyment of the following rights … the right to nationality.' In stories, people shared their experiences of considering the challenges of Article 8 of the European Convention on Human Rights (ECHR) – the right to respect for family and private life – as a strategy when they were unsure of their indefinite leave applications, thereby demonstrating how international human rights claims can bolster citizenship claims.

The *Nottebohm* case: acquiring nationality

A rather unusual illustration of when international law can intervene in nation-state conferred nationality can be found in the landmark *Nottebohm* case (*Liechtenstein v Guatemala*) [1955] ICJ 1), which was heard by the International Court of Justice (ICJ). Mr Nottebohm lived for many years in Guatemala, but he was a German national by origin. During the Second World War, he feared his German nationality would result in his being declared an enemy alien in Guatemala so he applied for citizenship of a different country, Lichtenstein, which was a neutral country in the war and had liberal naturalisation procedures. There was no requirement of residence in Lichtenstein, so Nottebohm obtained his nationality there and then he re-entered Guatemala. By that time, the US had entered the war and Guatemala had joined in alongside the US forces. Guatemala declared Nottebohm an enemy alien and refused to recognise the Lichtenstein nationality. Lichtenstein brought the complaint against Guatemala to the ICJ. The ICJ developed a legal test for nationality that required a real and effective connection with the nation state rather than a relationship of convenience. Nationality is the international dimension of citizenship. While international law rarely interferes with domestic citizenship requirements, it does have a role to play in the legal recognition of nationality. This decision meant Guatemala could refuse to recognise the Liechtensteinian nationality acquired by Nottebohm and Liechtenstein would not be able to provide him with diplomatic protection because of a lack of 'effective nationality'. Nottebohm's situation is an unusual one in the context of war and diplomatic protection, but it demonstrates that while acquisition of citizenship is a domestic matter, nationality has an outward-facing international dimension that can be affected by international law.

The *Rottmann* case: losing nationality

Another case in which the interaction between national citizenship and the supra-national framework was examined was the *Rottmann* case (Case C-135/08 *Janko Rottmann v Freistaat Bayern*) where the relationship between national citizenship and European Union (EU) citizenship was at stake. This relationship is only a few decades old as European citizenship was born in Maastricht on 7 February 1992, with the signing of the Treaty on European Union.[4] EU citizenship has often been equated with free movement as EU citizenship provides freedom from national immigration control and the right to move and reside freely within the territory of the member states (Article 21 of the Treaty on the Functioning of the EU). It also comes with certain rights attached that become stronger with time, eventually leading to national citizenship in the host country if host country nationality requirements are fulfilled. Apart from economic gains, EU institutions nurtured free movement and citizenship with the idea that freedom of movement can enhance feelings of belonging to the EU (Bellamy, 2008).

However, much exercise of EU citizenship has depended on individuals moving countries within the EU and there is a lack of clarity on whether EU citizenship rights can be wholly exercised without moving across member country borders.

A case where an individual did move borders and seek to change national citizenship is the *Rottmann* case. Rottmann was a citizen of Austria within the EU region, and he then applied for naturalisation in Germany. However, before he applied for German citizenship, he had committed fraud in Austria and a national warrant had been issued for him in that country. Rottmann should have disclosed this fraud or other crimes in his application form for the German nationalisation process, but he did not do so and the German authorities did not find out about the fraud until after Rottmann had been naturalised. Austrian domestic law immediately withdraws Austrian citizenship if someone acquires citizenship of another country and therefore Rottmann immediately lost his Austrian citizenship. When the German authorities found out about the fraud, they wanted to denaturalise Rottmann, but, in that case, he would be left without any surviving citizenship. The German government sought advice from the European Court of Justice (ECJ) on the issue as it was not sure what would happen to Rottmann in the circumstances.

The ECJ said that the significant legal contention here was not about national citizenship, or even about statelessness, but about EU citizenship, which depended on holding the citizenship of an EU country. If Rottmann had neither Austrian nor German citizenship left, he would also lose his EU community citizenship. Therefore, while the ECJ recognised national sovereignty over gain and loss of nationality and said that it is possible for loss of EU citizenship to take place as a result of loss of national citizenship, it also said that the proportionality test should be applied when EU citizenship is at stake. What this signifies is that only a grave breach of nationality requirements would probably justify interfering with EU citizenship.

International human rights law, the *Nottebohm* case, and the *Rottmann* case – are all 20th- and 21st-century developments that have reconfigured citizenship and nationality. To understand British citizenship, we need to step back a few centuries further and trace its origins from the days of subjecthood. At that time, national sovereignty over citizenship was largely unrestricted by formalised international rights and obligations.

The origins of British citizenship

Prior to 1707, Scotland and England were separate nations, and citizenship could only be Scottish or English. Despite the nations within its embrace being ancient ones, British citizenship is not found before 1707. It was only after 1707, when England and Scotland were unified, that one could be British. At that time, being British became about being born on British soil. This is the principle of *jus soli* (right of the soil), which establishes citizenship through connection by birth on the territory of a country regardless of parentage. Complexities arose when British fathers had children abroad. Clearly, there had to be some form of inclusionary rule for those children. The right to citizenship through descent from a British father became established in law to include children born in wedlock outside British territory, but limited to two generations. Children born outside who could claim citizenship through their blood-links in this manner exercised *jus sanguinis* (right of the blood). *Jus sanguinis* was used to supplement *jus soli* in order to expand British citizenry. Nationality can also be acquired through naturalisation.

In the days of empire, British subjects could all have equal, formal status as subjects by virtue of being equally subject to the authority of the Crown. The context in which citizenship operated was that of subjecthood to the Crown rather than as citizenship as it is understood today, with rights and duties exercisable in society. The 1914 British Nationality and Status of Aliens Act incorporated subjects into imperial subjects, local subjects and everyone else (aliens). There was disparity in the treatment meted out to these different kinds of subjects, as few subjects from abroad could afford to travel to the UK mainland. Although subjecthood in the imperial days was not an optional status for colonised people, it had two attractive features. First, British citizenship during days of empire and colonialism was, arguably, a rudimentary kind of transnational citizenship. Second, subjecthood was based on loyalty and allegiance towards the Crown, so, in theory, it was an equal status for all who were subjects. However, as this kind of political relationship was non-volitional, there was resentment in some colonies towards such citizenship.

Citizenship appeared as a category in the 1948 British Nationality Act because Britain had to respond to Canadian legislative changes that introduced a concept of Canadian citizenship as a prerequisite for British subjecthood. It was only in 1981 that the term British citizenship was introduced into statute because the right of abode was restricted to only British citizens by this change. Before then citizenship was only mentioned in terms of categories such as citizens of the UK and colonies, British subjects without citizenship, and citizens of Commonwealth countries, all of whom were called commonwealth citizens (Karatani, 2003). The change to a defined status of citizenship was in recognition of Britain no longer being an imperial power and, therefore, the emphasis shifted to finding blood-links to existing citizens for conferring citizenship.

After the two world wars, there was the forging of a new kind of citizenship. The colonies had fought side by side with Britain as part of the allied forces and so, with the decline of empire and the birth of newly independent states, a notion of a special status for former colonials emerged: Commonwealth citizenship. Again, this was not territorially limited to the UK, but embraced a number of regions in the world that were previously controlled by Britain. Complex rules of citizenship and immigration followed the decline of the British Empire and its transformation to the Commonwealth. Immigration into Britain was not regulated by law until the 18th century and, even thereafter, only in a very lax manner until the British colonies started gaining independence in the mid-20th century, so there was a steady inflow of migrants from different British colonies throughout this period. Many former colonial subjects in the various countries ruled by the British Empire were given the option of holding British passports after independence of the colonies. This was to continue their special historical connection with the Crown and to recognise the role of colonial support for Britain in both world wars. It enabled subject–citizens to continue to travel to the UK if they wanted to, and to reside and work there.

As African nations became self-governing, new problems emerged. African leaders in countries such as Uganda and Kenya sought to expel the ethnic minority Asians living there. These Asians held British passports and sought to enter the UK by virtue of this. Between 1966 and 1970, the Labour government took a decision to withdraw the right of entry from Asians with British passports who were driven out of Kenya. This proved to be very controversial. In *East African Asians v UK* – 4403/70 [1973] ECtHR 2 (14 December 1973), the European Court of Human Rights (ECtHR) found that the UK had acted incompatibly with Article 3 (the right to freedom from torture, inhuman and degrading treatment), Article 5 (the right to liberty), Article 8 (the right to respect for private and family life) and Article 14 (prohibition on discrimination) of the ECtHR.

This decision led to a complete overhaul of citizenship categories. Those East-African Asians who had retained their British citizenship were recategorised 'British overseas citizens' or 'British protected persons' under section 26 of the 1981 British Nationality Act. These statuses do not allow East-African Asians to live in the UK, so they no longer amount to full citizenship rights.

As already illustrated, the citizenship laws of each country dictate whether the country applies *jus soli* or *jus sanguinis* and explain the requirements for naturalisation. Until 1983, anyone born in the UK was automatically a citizen. The 1981 British Nationality Act secured British citizenship exclusively for those with close links to the UK, so now individuals acquire citizenship by birth on the territory provided their parents were 'legally settled' in the UK at the time of their birth. Modern British citizenship operates through a mix of territoriality and parentage.

Naturalisation: creating migrant–citizens

Naturalisation is the process for acquiring British citizenship when someone holds (or held) a foreign citizenship. In contemporary times it is the most prevalent route to citizenship, but in the past it was possible to naturalise only through separate, individual Acts of Parliament. This continued until 1844 (Brooks, 2016). Initially only Protestants from other lands were offered protection through this route, but naturalisation gradually embraced more long-term foreign residents. The 1914 Act laid down residency, 'good character' and language requirements for naturalisation. In 1975, the process for naturalisation was streamlined and no longer entailed separate Acts of Parliament. But modern naturalisation procedures still have components of residence and character as well as other formalised requirements, such as knowledge of culture, history and language, and a citizenship ceremony. Generally, adults have to evidence at least five years of residence in the UK, meet requirements of good character, have a certain level in language skills in English (or Welsh or Scottish Gaelic), and demonstrate 'knowledge of life in the UK' (as assessed by a 'Life in the UK' test, in the course of applying for settlement prior to the citizenship process). For children, the process is called registration rather than naturalisation and there are no requirements for language or knowledge tests. Instead, depending on the country of their birth and the nationalities of their parents, they may qualify for either automatic or discretionary 'registration' as British citizens.

Naturalisation provides the most immediate and visible connection between citizenship and migration. It infuses British society with diversity by bringing in people from all over the world. In 2016, 88 per cent of grants of citizenship were to non-EU nationals, which means that most new citizens come from countries with historical connections with Britain. The largest groups of newly naturalised UK citizens in 2016 had prior citizenship from India, Pakistan, Nigeria and South Africa, all countries that were part of the extended British Empire in the past. In 2016, a total of over 149,400 foreign nationals naturalised as British citizens in the three main categories: those who fulfil the five-year residency requirement; spouses and civil partners of British citizens; and underage children being registered as citizens. Nine per cent of citizenship applications were rejected in 2015 (Blinder, 2017). Most refusals are because of failure to meet requirements such as that of residence or that of 'good character'.

National identity and exclusion

The steps introduced, such as knowledge and language tests, for acquiring citizenship through naturalisation create a more invidious connection between citizenship and migration. This is through the deployment of 'national identity' in the application process. National identity is usually based on a presumed 'sameness' of values. Foreign-born migrants-turned-citizens are expected to incorporate elements of national identity and demonstrate these in the tests required for naturalisation. The English language ability and Life in the UK tests are examples of how national identity values enter the application process. Andreouli and Dashtipour (2014, p 100) write:

> Reforms in legislation concerning the process whereby migrants acquire British citizenship are part of a social cohesion agenda. These citizenship policies are linked to the politics of belonging and the management of national boundaries. This is evident in recent naturalisation legislation in the UK. Applicants for naturalisation, since 2005 and 2004 respectively, are required to pass a 'Life in the UK' test and attend a citizenship ceremony whereby they affirm or swear their allegiance to the Queen and pledge their loyalty to the UK.

These tests are not consciously plural in outlook; a monolithic view of history and culture generally permeates the facts and figures tested. These operate to legally exclude poorer or less educated migrants from non-English speaking countries (Ryan, 2008). Statistics show that migrants from poorer countries are much less likely to pass these tests (van Oers, 2014, p 183). Inability to meet English language requirements and the Life in the UK test bars potential applicants mainly from poorer countries or countries where the main language is not English. This fits in with the 'sorting' role of citizenship or the emphasis placed on 'earning one's right' (Andreouli and Dashtipour, 2014). Even if migrants pass the tests and become included in law as citizens, national identity and its presumption of sameness bias can still operate to exclude them from participation in society.

In the past, Britain largely rejected large-scale integration projects (Meer et al, 2010). Diversity meant providing equal opportunity to a diverse group of people who would live in mutual tolerance. However, with time the inclusion of ethnic minorities becomes dependent on establishing their sameness with majority attributes and calling for vocal condemnation of 'radicalism' or extremism (especially from Muslim migrants) (Meer and Modood, 2009).

Another explanation can be found in Benedict Anderson's work on 'imagined communities'. Anderson defined nations as imagined communities of fellow citizens. According to him, they are imagined communities 'because the members of even the smallest nation will never know most of their fellow-members, meet them, or even hear of them, yet in the minds of each lives the image of their communion' (Anderson, 2006 [1983], p 6). The 'imagined community' of the British state is one that consists of the majority ethnic citizenry and its values. Time and again, speeches by prominent politicians remind everyone that this is a 'Christian nation' or that British values do not permit certain cultural practices (see, for example, the then Prime Minister David Cameron's Christmas speech in 2015).[5] In 2006, the then Prime Minister Gordon Brown made a speech about Britishness being based not on ethnicity or race but, instead, on values such as respect for civic responsibilities, individual liberty and democratic equality.[6] However, these are liberal values rather than British values. The search for Britishness could be likened to the search for the mythical Holy Grail. It is never likely to end with a concrete set of values that will be widely accepted in the UK. Majoritarian values become proxy values for all. Bridget Anderson (2013) explains this through the manner in which immigration and citizenship operate to create categories of 'us' and 'them' in society. Majoritarian values are identified and consolidated as belonging to 'us', whereas the values held by 'them' attach to ethnic minorities present in the UK and observable as rarities. For instance, arranged marriages in British Asian families are often vilified as antithetical to British values of individual liberty because of assumptions about race (Wray, 2011, p 228). Migrants who become citizens, and sometimes second generations thereafter, may continue to remain one of 'them' through the operation of exclusionary politics linked to national identity – what Yuval-Davis (2011) calls the 'politics of belonging'.

The emphasis on sameness in the name of cohesion and integration denies the richness of diversity that contributes to British life. Perhaps this is a reason why after the referendum in 2016 on whether the UK should leave or remain in the EU, racial intolerance became heightened and people wearing headscarves were approached and asked to 'leave' by other members of public (Burnett, 2016; Guild, 2016).

National security: a new kind of citizenship?

Identity politics or the politics of belonging (in the form of exclusion) matters in everyday life, but comes to the fore in national security matters when minority community citizens are suspected of terrorism. Meer and colleagues (2010) write that immigration and asylum laws facilitate highly skilled immigration, while irregular migrants or asylum seekers are kept out through national security measures and treated as potential terrorists. Citizenship has also come in for scrutiny in UK courts in national security cases in the context of cancellation. A parliamentary briefing paper on deprivation of citizenship (Gower and McGuinness, 2017) reveals that a Home Office freedom of information response in June 2016 stated that there had been 81 deprivation of citizenship orders made in the years 2006-15. Thirty-six orders were about conduct not conducive to the public good. These are the ones most likely to be connected to national security. Generally, the cancellation order is challenged on the basis that the person who loses British citizenship has been rendered stateless. As statelessness is prohibited by international law, the challengers seek to establish the lack of alternative nationalities. An example of this in the UK is the *Pham* case. In *Pham v Secretary of State for the Home Department* [2015] UKSC 19, Pham was deprived of his British citizenship. Pham had arrived in the UK from Vietnam and had been a Vietnamese citizen at some point, but the question was whether his Vietnamese citizenship still survived. At that time, the British legislation did not permit the creation of statelessness, so it was critical that Pham had a surviving Vietnamese citizenship if he was to be deprived of his British one. Vietnamese officials declined to acknowledge that Pham was an existing national of Vietnam, but Vietnamese law on the point was unclear. The Supreme Court agreed with Pham that he was no longer Vietnamese, but had little to say about the substance of British citizenship.

Another case on national security and its effects on citizenship is *MM & GY & TY v Secretary of State for the Home Department* [2015] EWHC 3513 (Admin) where a woman and her two adult children were refused naturalisation solely because the husband (and father of the children) was believed to be associated with terrorism. The woman and children had fulfilled all naturalisation requirements themselves, yet the refusal letter stated:

> In light of your close association with an extremist, therefore, your application for naturalisation as a British citizen has been refused. The Home Secretary considers in particular that it is important to deter potential extremists from involvement in extremist activities, including by making it clear that any extremist activity could affect the immigration and nationality status of close members [of their family].

The court acknowledged in para 31 that there is wide discretion resting with the Home Secretary with regard to naturalisation matters. However, in this case, there was too wide a use of this discretion. The Home Secretary had not just focused on the good character of the applicant, but instead had looked into the 'the pursuit of broad and general public policy objectives' and, further, in para 40, the court stated:

> Severance might reflect more situations than the forcing apart of a family, since applicants might genuinely reject the activities and views of the family extremist, as it must be taken is the position here, and then also wish for nothing further to do with the family extremist.

These cases related to national security have brought to the fore the effect of conduct on citizenship. National security concerns have (arguably) created a new creature of law – a revocable citizenship – and also introduced additional scrutiny for naturalisation. Legislative change in 2014 (the 2014 Immigration Act) has now made it possible to render naturalised citizens stateless should they act 'in a manner which is seriously prejudicial to the vital interests of the United Kingdom, any of the Islands, or any British overseas territory'. This is possible if the Home Secretary 'has reasonable grounds to believe that the person is able to become a national of another country or territory under its laws', but the person may have no other existing nationality. Statelessness is thus a real possibility now. These changes affect applicants seeking naturalisation or naturalised citizens much more than any other kind of citizen because they are the ones who can face additional scrutiny on conduct for applications and also be rendered stateless despite achieving citizenship. While it is likely that very few successful applicants worry about this aspect (as they consider themselves safe from such rarely used measures), naturalised citizens remain susceptible as a category to cancellation that may render them stateless. Arguably, British citizenship is no longer an equal legal status even in a narrow formal sense.

Categorical exclusion

Categories have often been used to exclude people with claims to citizenship rights in the past as well. For example, Asians in East Africa were often referred to as refugees when they were British 'protected' persons or British overseas citizens. Many were refused entry into Britain as these statuses were murky in law and not considered the equivalent of full citizenship. In *Thakrar v Secretary of State for the Home Department* [1974] 2 All ER 261 (CA), Thakrar, a person of Asian origin born in Uganda, claimed that he was a protected person within the meaning of the 1948 British Nationality Act. Independence in 1962 meant that Ugandan citizenship was optional and, on taking that option, protected personage status ceased. It is unclear on facts whether Thakrar opted for Ugandan citizenship, but he was expelled from Uganda in 1972 as he was of Asian heritage. Thakrar claimed that he was still a protected person and as such the same as a UK citizen with a right to live in the UK. He claimed that, as he never made a formal declaration renouncing his protected person status, he retained such status. The Court of Appeal disagreed with Thakrar, finding that even if he were a protected person, he would have needed leave under section 3(1) of the 1971 Immigration Act. A protected person who had never lived in the UK did not automatically have a right to settle. This means Thakrar, who had no means of living in Uganda, could not enter into the UK either, despite his status as a British protected person. The case exemplifies the difficulties with operationalising the rights granted by various British immigration and nationality categories and how people are excluded by categories.

On the other hand, categories of inclusion have also changed over time. One such example is of the decline of Commonwealth citizenship as a category of legal rights. Commonwealth citizens had special rights of entry in the past, but this has gradually diminished. Yet, Commonwealth citizens still retain the right to vote in national elections. Their status is different from that of other nationals, as explained by Lord Diplock in *Director of Public Prosecutions Appellant v Bhagwan Respondent [On Appeal from Regina v Bhagwan]* [1972] AC 60 HL:

In 1962 the relevant distinction between Commonwealth citizens and aliens as respects entry to the United Kingdom was that all Commonwealth citizens could, but aliens could not, enter the United Kingdom without anyone's leave at whatever place they chose. If it had been desired in either of these respects to assimilate Commonwealth citizens, to whom the Act applied, to aliens the legislative precedent was ready to the draftsman's hand in article 1 of the Aliens Order 1953, which I have previously cited. Parliament's failure to follow that precedent strongly suggests a legislative intention that Commonwealth citizens, even though liable to exclusion from the United

Kingdom, should be subject to a less rigorous control upon their entry than that which in 1962 was imposed upon aliens.

While Commonwealth status is relatively weak as a source of legal rights in modern times, it still has a privileged position.

Illegitimacy as an example of categorical exclusion

Illegitimacy of birth is a prominent example of categorical exclusion that exists because of outdated provisions in nationality law. Stories in this book indicate how people born out of wedlock are sometimes categorically excluded from British citizenship. While marriage of parents no longer matters if the mother is British, it continues to make a difference if the father is a certain kind of British national from overseas territories and the mother is not British. Children born to them out of wedlock are not entitled to automatic British citizenship. This is an aberration to the general principle of equality and non-discrimination upheld in recent decision of the Supreme Court for children born to unmarried parents. In *R (on the application of) Johnson v Secretary of State for the Home Department* [2016] UKSC 5, discrimination on grounds of illegitimacy was found to be unjustified when it fell within the ambit of the right to respect for private life and family life (Articles 8 and 14 of the ECHR). Johnson was born in Jamaica in 1985 and moved to the UK aged four. His father was a British citizen, but was not married to Johnson's mother, and so could not pass on his citizenship under the relevant laws of the time. Johnson was convicted of manslaughter in 2008 and sentenced to nine years' imprisonment. The facts in *Johnson* are about deportation, but the issue of deportation came up because Johnson was treated as foreign despite having lived nearly all his life in Britain. Lady Hale gave the only substantive judgment, but it was held, unanimously, that Johnson's liability to deportation as a result of his illegitimacy was unlawful discrimination in breach of the ECHR.

Despite this case, and other legislative changes that have brought in gender equality in citizenship acquisition, if the father is not a full British citizen but is a different kind of British national, such as a

British overseas territories citizen, he is still not able to pass on British nationality to children born out of wedlock. One person affected by this situation who shared his story of campaigning for reform in this area is Mr Miller,[7] who was born in the US in 1969. His father was born in Montserrat, which was then a British colony and is now a British overseas territory. Through several legislative reclassifications Mr Miller's father was categorised as a British overseas territories citizen who would have had full entitlement to status as a British citizen. The sole reason he could not pass on this citizenship status to Mr Miller, however, was because he was not married to Mr Miller's mother and the reform in law on legitimacy and acquisition of nationality did not extend to those born to British overseas territories citizens. Mr Miller explains how the inability to access British citizenship affects him personally, as follows:

"This eats away at the core of one's own identity. To be shut out from officially claiming and enjoying your father's heritage, to be denied the right to be recognized is simply downright wrong."

Mr Miller's story illustrates how the piecemeal nature of reform in nationality legislation leads to continued categorical discrimination against people who identify as British and have close links to the UK.

Conclusion

This chapter has traced some key developments in British citizenship and nationality over time and presented the general conceptual framework of citizenship theory through selected examples. The example of birth out of wedlock as a categorical exclusion serves to underline some vital points that are developed further in subsequent chapters. The categories of different kinds of nationalities contained within British nationality provisions, and the differing content of rights attached to each status, are of continued relevance in contemporary times. Legal analyses of these categories are mostly devoid of the context of individual experiences of citizenship. Mr Miller's words connect formal legal citizenship with a more substantive understanding of citizenship as identity or belonging. Ending this chapter with Mr Miller's personal story marks a transition point in this book. From now on, the book shifts from formal legal developments, with more abstract and distanced conceptual theorising, to understanding the experiences of those who are affected by the laws directly from their own words and through their own perceptions. The reasons for this transition form the subject matter of Chapter Two, which is a brief introduction to storytelling as a research methodology.

TWO

British citizenship and migration in stories

"For me, citizenship is my blue suitcase which I lugged from one meeting to another. Filled with papers. Birth certificate, mortgage loan papers, you name it. My whole life – in a box. For every lawyers' meeting. And of course, the lawyer always wanted the one bit of paper I did not have that time. It was mad, the amount of papers I had in that box for 6-8 years. I still have that blue suitcase, but I do not take it on trips." (Adaoma, a 54-year-old Nigerian-born woman, trained physiotherapist based in Bristol)

Why tell stories of migration?

What does Adaoma's account here bring to mind? Perhaps the image of a blue suitcase stuffed with papers documenting her life? One can almost feel the weight of the suitcase, the immense burden of its contents. One can experience Adaoma's emotions of frustration and disappointment and feel for her relentless efforts to make law work, culminating in the suitcase as a memento of success. All of these permeate Adaoma's account and reach us directly. Herein lies the strength of a narrative approach to the law and legal process: the ability to reach into people's lived experiences of the law and gain an enhanced understanding of the capacity of law, as well as its hurdles.

Without storytelling, law is a dry subject, lifeless and dispassionate. Hiding behind legal reasoning and objectivity, as well as neutral standards devoid of context, law becomes a meaningless, technical exercise that has little to do with how ordinary people live and experience it. Although cases contain stories of how disputes arise and reach court, law remains inaccessible to most non-lawyers in their everyday lives as its stories are obscured in legalism.

Narratives in law

Why then is the legal format so distant in tone? There is a deep suspicion of emotions and images in law. The presumption is that anything not dispassionate in tone is likely to cloud judgment. Pictures and images can evoke more emotions than text and are therefore viewed with greater suspicion than written text. A non-narrative, third-person account is lofty in nature and so more authoritative and impartial, maintaining a distance from the immediate problems of litigants. Unsurprisingly, the visceral impact of the law on the senses, emotions and reasoning of people is largely filtered out from legal texts.

Law searches for some account of truth in its processes. This truth is linked to conceptions of justice and is to be found via these legal processes. It is 'objectively' out there. The search for the truth and the need to preserve authority over its 'subjects' are important goals in law's empire. The tone of law sets its boundaries. Prior to entering the legal domain, there is a cloakroom where those subject to the law hang the parts of their lives amputated by law. Only then are they given entry as proper 'legal subjects' who can search for justice. For that reason, the power of stories cannot be ignored, especially in juxtaposition with legal reports. Levit (2009, p 263) explains this as follows:

> Stories are one of the primary ways that humans understand situations. People remember events in story form. Stories illuminate diverse perspectives; they evoke empathic understanding; and their vivid details engage people in ways that sterile legal arguments do not.

Stories form the arc that connects the macro field of politics and the micro field of social behaviour.[8]

Storytelling in law

While law and doctrinal legal scholarship continue to operate in this selective manner, two developments have changed the academic terrain around lived experiences and storytelling in law in recent years. First, legal academics, particularly those interested in race or in gender, have sought to go beyond this game of distance and objectivity. Scholars in critical race theory, feminist theory and social justice lawyering recognise the importance of storytelling in bringing in the voice of the marginalised (Futrell, 2015). Second, scholars of legal pedagogy find that law school teaching and learning is enhanced through storytelling (both drawing on real case law and data, as well as hypothetical situations). In law clinic and legal ethics classes the dominant pedagogy is challenged through stories (Shanks, 2007; Krieger and Martinez, 2010; Whalen-Bridge, 2010). The scholars of 'alternative' pedagogy have analysed the suspicion of 'untruths' in stories, and this equates to the suspicion in law of the 'subversive subject' who is usually not white or male or privileged in terms of class. Thus, storytelling has taken on a new significance in legal scholarship of late. An example can be found in the feminist judgments project where court cases have been rewritten by scholars to reflect feminist jurisprudence (Hunter et al, 2010).[9]

Two specific movements have brought storytelling to the fore: the law and literature movement (Chestek, 2012), and applied legal storytelling, which focuses on how lawyers and judges use stories in justifying arguments (Edwards, 2009). The law and literature movement looks for images of law in literature and traces of literature in law, whereas the applied legal storytelling movement looks for stories behind the use of legal authority, policy and principle. An example of law and literature approaches to storytelling and citizenship can be found in Janice Ho's book *Nation and citizenship in the twentieth-century British novel* (2015). Ho traces images of British citizenship down the ages in leading British novels. Applied storytelling can be found in many areas of law, but, in certain areas of law, such as constitutional law where the macro structures of society matter in law, legal cases generally tell stories about the larger context, thereby moving away from the private realm of storytelling and into the political and social realms. Storytelling in law cases is not smooth or sleek as in novels, because law separates out facts and principles in its own distinct way. But it exists nevertheless in a rather stylised and formalised legal narrative. Paula Abrams (2007) points out that appellate opinions that do not review the factual merits of cases generally have the least amount of factual scrutiny. As these cases concentrate on narrow questions of laws, they generally have the most formalistic tone focusing on legal doctrine.

Carrie Menkel-Meadow (2000) sets out the constraints within which lawyers or law teachers can use stories. First, the veracity of the story matters. Second, there has to be abundant information about the storyteller or narrator (author, teacher, student, lawyer, client).

Third, there has to be enough information to understand the context from which to analyse a decision made. Once these three factors are satisfied, the stories should present learning opportunities of a kind not available from merely reading texts of law, which are abstract and distilled through legal reasoning.

Giving voice

Storytelling is particularly effective for including accounts from marginalised people or bringing forth untold narratives and memories from the past. Richard Delgado (1989, p 2412) writes:

> Many, but by no means all, who have been telling legal stories are members of what could be loosely described as outgroups, groups whose marginality defines the boundaries of the mainstream, whose voice and perspective – whose consciousness – has been suppressed, devalued, and abnormalised. The attraction of stories for these groups should come as no surprise. For stories create their own bonds, represent cohesion, shared understandings, and meanings. The cohesiveness that stories bring is part of the strength of the outgroup. An outgroup creates its own stories, which circulate within the group as a kind of counter-reality.

Similarly, storytelling also makes room for presenting collective accounts that may transcend individual ones, if it is carried out in a group storytelling session or if it seeks accounts of people's social networks (Eastmond, 2007).

Delgado (1989, p 2413) says that 'Stories, parables, chronicles, and narratives are powerful means for destroying mindset', while other scholars have pointed out that the narrative power of stories is also used for majoritarian agendas, including stories of national pride that seek to exclude those who are different in any manner. Peter Brooks and Paul Gewirtz (1998, pp 46-7) argue that because pornography and hate speech also contain stories, they need to be countered in order to gain a measure of control over these issues. While this is true, majoritarian agendas usually have many outlets (including stories), while marginalised accounts have few. Thus, stories are more important for bringing to life marginalised accounts that are often unable to cross the barriers of legal research, reasoning and writing.

Stories as data: example from legal consciousness

The point remains that stories cannot be embraced as data without critical thought being given to their research value. As Menkel-Meadow (2000) mentions, it is important to have adequate information to check the veracity of stories. Stories can be tested for internal validity by looking for patterns across multiple accounts. Stories can also be verified for external validity and veracity by cross-checking against other kinds of data. Legislative sources, reported judgments and reports of other research accounts can all be marshalled to fortify the narrative accounts in storytelling. Once stories are triangulated against other data and also examined for patterns, they are of greater value as empirical data. However, as with any other data, stories should not be treated as proxies for an 'objective truth' that can somehow be determined through rigorous analysis. To engage in complex analysis is to acknowledge that data is indicative of connections rather than determinative of causality in most social-scientific situations.

Similarly, stories can help improve the validity of other kinds of data. For instance, relying on accounts in reported law (legislation and case law) as standalone data sources leaves out numerous dimensions that may be relevant for answering research questions. Greta Olson (2014) writes that legal texts have a distinct manner of presentation of facts, more useful for purposes of legal reasoning and the expression of abstract norms than for providing a sense of the person behind the text. The voice of law is a neutral disembodied one that seldom engages with the emotions or sentiments of the characters in its narrations. Scholars who seek to go beyond the law look for other kinds of narratives that law normally suppresses. A prime example is legal consciousness literature where storytelling data is considered to be of critical importance. Dave Cowan (2004, p 929) writes:

Legal consciousness research seeks to understand people's routine experiences and perceptions of law in everyday life. The focus above all, then, is on subjective experiences, rather than on, for example, law and its effects in society.

And in Ewick and Silbey's (1998) landmark book on legal consciousness, *The common place of law*, storytelling introduces the personal into the legal, highlighting the ways in which law matters to people.

Bringing people and their experiences to the forefront is particularly relevant for the field of migration and citizenship studies where there is a dichotomy between two major kinds of studies: first, legal studies of migration and nationality laws, which are focused on doctrine; and, second, the empirically grounded approach of geographers, sociologists, political scientists and anthropologists in documenting people's migration journeys and lives. As a result, how people experience law in their lives while migrating is nearly always a silent script running in the background of other analyses of their life situations. To foreground those experiences of the law, we need stories such as Adaoma's. Adaoma's first-person account tells us what law meant to her. The other stories in this book will also underline the capacity of law, as well as its ability to set up barriers for migrants. But, more importantly, stories reach into emotional depths that cannot be plumbed by other kinds of data. This is critical for understanding aspects of citizenship, such as belonging, where increasingly the complexities are about the emotive components of people's lives rather than merely their physical dislocations.

The visual turn

Suspicion of storytelling is not limited only to words. It also includes visual representations such as pictures and photographs. James Parry Eyster (2008, p 87) quotes the renowned jurist Oliver Wendell Holmes Jr as saying: 'Of course, the law is not the place for the artist or the poet'. Holmes's words demonstrate the suspicion of images and words in legal scholarship. This is because law is supposedly about reasoning, whereas stories, poetry and images may tug at people's emotions. The suspicion of the visual has operated to keep visual representations of the law to the minimum. Pictures, often conflated with cartoon images, are considered infantile and over-simplistic representations that have no place in the sophisticated world of modern law.

Recent research has, however, taken a turn towards including the visual in the law and freed law from mere textual analysis. For instance, in 2017 the UK Socio-Legal Studies Association held its annual conference on the theme of images of law. The plenary address at the meeting by Linda Mulcahy, Thomas Giddens and Amanda Perry-Kessaris focused on the visual in law and the importance of visually representing research.[10] A number of socio-legal scholars now work on using drawing and graphic media for legal studies and in using storytelling for giving direct voice to actors who experience law. In legal consciousness research, the importance of objects in legal consciousness is also a new development. In this discipline, scholars track case files to demonstrate the role of objects as actors (van Oorschot and Schinkel, 2015). For citizenship research, the use of material objects such as clothing, photographs and mementoes can concretise abstract collective histories, traditions and cultures, such as 'nationhood' (Skey, 2011; May, 2013). These developments of multiple dimensions of legal research provide an exciting opportunity to present people without them being disembodied by the disinterested gaze of the law.

Why stories of citizenship?

The trend towards tightening formal processes (such as difficult tests) forms part of the experiences narrated by many citizenship applicants. However, the emotions of belonging appear to drive how people perceive the formal processes. Further, many applicants think British law is fundamentally fair, but its application is the problem. From applicants' stories it is possible to identify the gaps between legal provisions and their implementation, as well as the more restrictive and conditional turns that afflict British citizenship in contemporary times.

The folkloric narrative format is suitable for citizenship research as such research has lately moved away from a focus on identity and integration towards understanding the relational and emotive belonging of migrants. The stories in this book demonstrate an affective understanding of belonging in contemporary British society that is often challenged by the hardships of acquiring the formal legal status of citizenship. For applicants, belonging is fundamental to citizenship and belonging is not just about inclusion or exclusion (the politics of belonging). It is a deep emotion connected to inner sensations of 'home', as well as attachment to specific places.

An example of the folkloric format can be found in Elspeth Guild's work (2016). Guild uses the image of the monster and the monstrous form to analyse EU citizenship in the UK. The monster is a folkloric character who symbolises a problem or a failed project. The metaphorical framework helps readers understand what happened to the EU project in the UK.

Use of storytelling in this book

Most of the data in this book is from a project on British citizenship funded by the Economic and Social Research Council. The project focuses on long-term residents on the pathways to citizenship. Interviews were conducted with several long-term residents who had successfully become citizens after initially arriving in the UK for their jobs or education. Interviews were also conducted with lawyers who work on nationality applications. Some respondents were contacted via their lawyers while others were recruited through events on migration and citizenship. Some were referrals from initial interviewees. Overall, there were 30 participants. The conversations with the successful citizenship applicants were semi-structured but largely free-flowing discussions. The storytellers were given minimum guidance in terms of what they should talk about: broadly their citizenship in terms of the legal process and other aspects they considered important. But people were asked to include some visual or other sensory impression linked to citizenship in order to focus their narrative. Some stories are developed from initial interviews. The interview questions were open-ended and the topics were on migration pathways to the UK, significant landmarks and impressions of residence in the UK, the decision to naturalise, the legal process of naturalisation, overall identity and belonging, as well as the meaning of British citizenship.

The participants who shared their stories are from the most popular countries of origin for naturalisation in the UK representing each continent. Most are represented in the top ten countries of origin (for example, India, Pakistan, Nigeria, South Africa, Zimbabwe and Ghana), as well as from EU member states (about 12 per cent of citizenship grants in 2016 were to EU nationals). Stories were gathered at storytelling events and were also tracked from online immigration advisory boards. In the online boards, applicants discussed their citizenship procedures and sought advice from fellow applicants. Stories and interviews were analysed for dominant themes using the approach popularised by Braun and Clarke (2006, p 79), which involves 'identifying, analysing, and reporting patterns (themes) within the data'.

Most of the storytellers in this book are professional workers or people who entered along with professional workers on dependent visas. Some of them entered the UK on ancestral visas. Ancestral visas are available for nationals of Commonwealth countries who can claim descent from British-born grandparents. Some of the other storytellers are individuals who sought asylum in the UK. Most storytellers have lived close to a decade in the UK, although some have lived here much longer and some for slightly shorter durations of time.

While there is tremendous diversity in race, ethnicity and class, as well as in pathways, there are some significant similarities in how the applicants experienced and dealt with the law and legal processes and how they reflected on their own citizenship trajectories (and lives) after the processes had ended. Bureaucracy and expense, for instance, were omnipresent themes in the stories of both Commonwealth citizens and those from the European Economic Area (EEA). During Brexit discussions concerning the UK's planned withdrawal from the European Union, the position of EEA nationals who apply for British citizenship has become less secure and their experience has started mirroring those of migrants from elsewhere. Over 2016-17, therefore, research themes have converged even more owing to the Brexit negotiations.

The research started with an assumption that successful applicants would perceive citizenship as a legal status or relationship because they would have direct experience of its legal dimensions. True, the expectation was that they would have other ideas about citizenship as well, but their encounters with nationality provisions, often after many years of experiencing immigration law, would surely privilege a legalistic vision of law that would match the state-centric image of citizenship. Research findings seldom fit expectations, however. While people who were successful applicants did discuss the legal process and the salience of the law in *becoming* citizens, they did not dwell on these in terms of *being* citizens. During in-depth interviews of about 90 minutes' duration (on average), the stories about being citizens related more to people's pasts and memories, motivations for migration, early experiences and the match with expectations than to the requirements of nationality law. Interviewees and participants were asked to describe an object, visual image, or distinct memory (for instance, a particular foodstuff) associated with citizenship and these descriptions provide the visual elements to the narratives. Adaoma's blue suitcase has its own value in storytelling by capturing what is not recorded in official transcripts.

Conclusion

In this book, the chapter headings are based on different kinds of storytelling formats, such as folklores/folktales, myths, legends and fairy tales (Bascom, 1965). These are all forms of storytelling that set out some moral principles but generally transcend both time and place. Folklores consist of stories of origins and tales that are beyond specific times or places. For this reason, Chapter Three sets out folkloric accounts of citizenship and thereby tries to transcend the time and place parameters of the migrant–citizen experience and uncover accounts of why migrants choose to become citizens. It is about people's perspectives on citizenship and belonging and focuses on their overall citizenship journey. Transcending particularistic elements through storytelling is possible because in every culture and place people enjoy stories that strike a chord with them. Similarly, myths and legends are usually stories of battles and beginnings. Chapter Four on myths and legends offers accounts of struggle and ritualistic elements of the citizenship applications. These form the explanations for how people become citizens. Both Chapters Four and Five are about the application process, but Chapter Five – entitled 'Fairy tales?' – recounts the narratives of self-affirmation and success through the citizenship journey. There are some elements of these stories that even the narrators themselves find difficult to believe as they are 'dreamlike' in quality like the fairy tales themselves. In all the chapters there is an element of the real mixed with the fictive as migration is as much about forging new identities and aspirations as it is about re-examining past lives with nostalgia and longing. People view themselves and others through prisms of heroism and historicity in a manner that is folkloric as well as real. Symbolism and fantasy are real to those who make the citizenship journey.

Chapter Six is the conclusion of the book. It highlights research findings and proposes policy recommendations for addressing the hurdles encountered by applicants.

THREE

A folkloric account of citizenship and belonging

The previous two chapters were foundational ones that laid out key developments, premises and methodological aspects of the book. This chapter focuses on the stories of applicants who present their perceptions and views on British citizenship and belonging. The succeeding two chapters assess the links between the citizenship application process and people's sense of belonging.

Citizenship from the eyes of citizens

State-centric accounts of formal, legal citizenship abound in reports and academic texts on citizenship. State law on citizenship is primarily about the attachment of rights and duties to an individual that are subsequent to arrival, entry and settlement in a country. Do individual applicants portray citizenship in the same manner? How do they describe citizenship, its processes and its parameters? This chapter evaluates to what extent their portrayals match state accounts or explanations written by scholars on citizenship.

As previously mentioned, folklores or folktales are morality tales that transcend time and space. These are useful for capturing the main elements of narrative in citizenship accounts. The stories are folkloric accounts of citizenship and belonging because, although they are about specific places and times, they are also about the more universal story of migration, whenever or wherever the migration may take place. It is about setting up home in foreign lands, wherever they be located, down the ages.

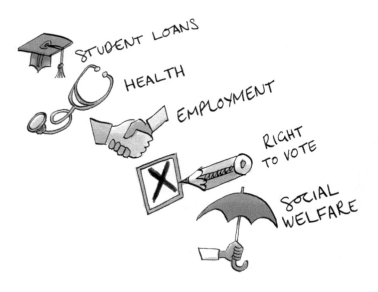

The stories people share depend in content on many factors, including their entry pathways to Britain, their countries of origin, and their length of period of residence in Britain. Nationals from outside the European Economic Area (EEA) have become citizens after acquiring indefinite leave to remain (ILR), a settled status from which one can proceed to citizenship and which enables one to change employers. EEA nationals become citizens after acquiring permanent settlement, a status very similar to ILR from which they can proceed to British citizenship.

While this chapter explores at length what citizenship means in terms of people's own perceptions, it seems important at the outset to briefly set out some broad themes that emerge from the stories. The topics that dominated the stories people narrated were about what made them feel British or what set them apart from holding British 'values'. Also central to the narratives were associations with the past or the break from those connections, and the retention of multiple identities or the inability to incorporate more than one. People describe their social networks, family connections and work lives at length. Moreover, they deploy several linguistic strategies to describe the emotions attached to changing locations and becoming rooted. They often channel emotions and memories connected with their migration journeys through visual images. These accounts, which give a more visceral account of citizenship, are usually invisible in the formal, legal, state-centric analysis of British citizenship and nationality laws and procedures. Overall, from the accounts of the applicants, a complex relationship of affinity between belonging and citizenship can be established.

Scottish or not? British or not?

"Kilts, haggis, all those things … yes those are special for me as Scots. A lot of my family I define as Scottish but I am British. I've, obviously, lived in Newport for many years.… Then it's been funny, in the last couple of years talking with my family, with the Scottish independence coming up, and then what that would mean to my British identity, because I kind of specifically identify with being British. So, what does that mean like if Scotland breaks away? It's a weird idea of like, legally, your citizenship, but also then because we as a family still have that identity of Scottish, I spent a lot of time in Edinburgh as a child, and like that's kind of where I still belong … that was a weird kind of feeling, yes. But then I think of Andy Murray going through the same thing, playing for GB everywhere, and now what with indyref [independence referendum] he doesn't really know does he! Same as me, and many others…. Asking 'Who am I'?"[11]

This account provided by James, a Cardiff-based computer scientist, demonstrates a few key points about how individuals reflect on citizenship and belonging. Instead of looking at citizenship in terms of the state or in terms of the rights and duties of the individual, like James, most people find they relate to citizenship in terms of their own identity and sense of belonging. James elaborates on identity and belonging in terms of significant relationships (strong ties), memories (objects and neighbourhoods associated with childhood are especially important) and place-belonging (current location or place of long-term residence). All of these will be developed further through other citizenship stories in this chapter.

For now, let us remain with James's story. James was not just conflicted about the independence referendum in Scotland. He has had other struggles with citizenship in his life. He was born in Nairobi when his father was working there as an engineer and then lived there for five years before returning to the UK. His father was Scottish but his mother was Austrian. His parents remained unmarried, separating while he was still very young. He was not close to his mother or her family and was brought up by his father in Scotland.

Everyone presumed James was legally British; there was no reason to think otherwise. But one day James found out that, in fact, he was not automatically British. This is because of historical discrimination in British nationality laws that prevented British unmarried fathers from passing on British citizenship to their children born abroad (a topic covered in brief in Chapter One). James found this out only when he applied for a passport to go on a school ski trip to France at age 15. It was a shock.

Eventually, James was able to register as a British citizen. In time, legislative change removed this discrimination against children born to their unwed British fathers, but at that time, waiting to go on a fun ski trip, it was utterly bewildering for James to find out that he had to undergo a special legal process to become British. Even this process may not have been available to him but for the ingenious strategic interventions made on his behalf by his lawyer.

Growing up as he did in Edinburgh, James had never considered himself a foreigner amid his Scottish family members. As Mary Gilmartin and Bettina Migge (2015) point out, ancestry and family relationships are the primary factors that create belonging, and, for James, both of these were predominantly British. Autobiographical factors connect him to specific British places and to particular British people so the legal situation was a mismatch with his life experiences (Dixon and Durrheim, 2004, p 459).

Just as we see with James, childhood memories are critical for most people in discussing their sense of personal identity (Fenster, 2005, pp 247-8). The state is still not a central presence for him, despite his experience with the law. This is surprising as the encounter with state agents and agencies is prominent at the time of his application for citizenship. Yet, James did not dwell on those points, but, instead, remembered his school friends and teachers and their surprise at discovering he did not have a means of getting a passport. While he is unclear as to what his legal status was when he first entered the country as a child, he recollects vividly the pain of seeing everyone else leaving for the ski trip without him. Again, the state and rights or duties were not salient to his story.

Citizenship theories in academic literature

How does James's account match up to accounts of citizenship in citizenship literature? When we look at scholarship on citizenship, the predominant image of citizenship is of reciprocal rights and duties. Liberal theory largely fails to account for relational aspects of citizenship. The state and the individual are the mainstays of liberal

accounts of rights and duties, but other intermediary relationships are generally absent (Kymlicka, 1995).

In republican theories of citizenship, there is an idea of the political community that is intermediary to the individual and the state (Dagger, 2002). However, again, the focus of relationships between actors is on rights that can be claimed and duties that are owed. In republican theories, the idea of responsibilities is more expansive. Individuals who speak of citizenship, however, do not appear to unpack it as a set of responsibilities towards nation building or as an obligation for the maintenance of the nation state.

Communitarian theories of citizenship view citizens as not just part of political communities but as integral to the communities themselves (Kymlicka and Norman, 1994). According to communitarian theories, individuals are relationally located in society instead of being atomised bearers of rights and duties. This view of citizenship resonates most with the perceptions of citizenship applicants who tend to identify citizenship in terms of their societal relations and their spatial locations. However, people are also inclined to include more affective and descriptive elements in their accounts that add different complexions to citizenship theories. It is not just in individual applicant stories that these variations can be found. Janice Ho (2015, p 14) finds similar shifts while examining images of citizenship in British novels. She writes in her book *Nation and citizenship in the twentieth-Century British novel* that 'narratives of citizenship expand the scope of what is thinkable in terms of the rights and responsibilities of citizenship that can be demanded from or enjoined by the state'.

A liberal rights and duties model of citizenship is pertinent to some extent for people in the matter of voting and the influence of voting on motivations for applying for citizenship. Many people consider voting as a key reason for their application. A Scottish report on refugees who became citizens (Stewart and Mulvey, 2011) found that people felt powerless as refugees and were eager to be politically involved through voting once they obtained citizenship. One person, GM15, noted that 'the freedom of a citizen … you have a freedom to vote and to … make your own, position on who you like to vote to, cause, like for us we are refugees and we are not entitled to vote or to participate in politics or something like this in the country' (quoted in Stewart and Mulvey, 2011, p 36). Another, GF8, stated that 'when you're a refugee you can't like participate in things like voting', while GM5 stated, 'for sure, there is a great difference between being a refugee and a British. To be a British is the best, because a person will be able to take part in the election and travel easily. For example, now I cannot take part in the election' (2011, p 36). While voting is an individual right, it is exercised in order to participate in society so to that extent it is a relational right. GM18 explained:

> ... and the thing that also come with being a citizen is that you are able to vote. I never had that chance in my country. It's something that I do cherish, you know, having...being able to actually vote and feel that my vote will be counted. That's a very important...and I thought it was, yeah, something that, you know, I had to do. (Quoted in Stewart and Mulvey, 2011, p 39)

Similarly, on an immigration advisory board online, a British citizen of American origin said: 'I became a British citizen in 2010, primarily so that I could vote. As we say in my country of origin, "No taxation without representation".'[12] Several EEA nationals who were excluded from voting in the 2016 referendum on whether the UK should remain in the European Union were similarly keen to apply for British citizenship in order to vote in the general election.[13] In later stories of migrant–citizens we find more accounts of how important political participation is for would-be citizens.

Absence of the state in individual narratives

For James, the state was not a relevant actor in citizenship. He is not an exception in emphasising micro relations over macro relations while telling stories of citizenship. In 30 transcripts of stories of citizenship the word 'state' appears merely twice, although several people refer to the 'government' (nearly 50 references) or 'country' (65 references).

Some people use 'government' as a proxy for state machinery, although generally they use it to discuss a policy or political intervention that is relevant to their story. 'Country' is used in a more generic sense to discuss the origin and routes of migration, as well as location of current residence, so its analytical value as a concept is rather limited.

The absence of state in individual stories maps well with ideas of communitarian citizenship. T. H. Marshall, the well-known communitarian theorist of citizenship, does not mention the state in his classical definition of citizenship as being 'full membership of the community, with all its rights and responsibilities' (1950, p 8). Local communities, especially cities and neighbourhoods, are more important in people's accounts of citizenship than an abstraction of a distant 'state'. However, arguably, perceptions of state are hidden in the use of terms such as 'the law' and 'legal process', which are sometimes used in the sense of state power or governance. An example is available from Mani's story of citizenship. Mani is a British citizen of Sri Lankan origin working as an engineer in London. He said:

"The law sides with the employer so you can't change jobs. The law keeps you tied and it is a feeling of slavery although you get paid. Until I got ILR [indefinite leave to remain] the law did not assist me in any way. I was constantly stressed. The legal process – in quite a planned way – is made that way. I did not have any job security and did not know how long I could stay in England until I got my ILR. Years of worrying for me, my family, it's really not fair."

The repeated use of the term 'law' in this story and the agency attributed to law roughly fits the profile of 'state' or 'state power'.

If the state is not, directly, the focus of individual narratives, what then dominates the accounts? From James's story, we can see that James had a clear sense of belonging before he acquired formal legal status as citizen. His citizenship is an emotion generated from his association with communities and neighbourhoods. Other stories similarly recount anecdotes of family, friendships and workplace rather than dwelling on the legal rights and duties of citizenship. The significance of the predominance of relations and locations in stories signifies that for applicant–citizens a sense of belonging is the critical element of citizenship, rather than, for example, passport holding or legal procedures.

What is belonging?

Perhaps this is a good point to pause and think of the differences between 'belonging' and 'citizenship' as both terms are connected but cover different elements. John Crowley (1999, p 22) writes that belonging is a 'thicker' concept than citizenship because it has more ingredients than citizenship. Marco Antonsich (2010) calls belonging a 'sense of rootedness', among other emotions. Anne McNevin (2006) and Christina Getrich (2008) specify that there are three main components of political belonging: first, economic belonging; second, social belonging; and, third, universal belonging. Economic belonging is achieved when immigrants are fully part of the economy. When immigrants participate in everyday social relations and exchanges, they have social belonging, and, when immigrants draw on human rights to make claims for their presence, they demonstrate universal belonging (Bhabha, 1999, p 21; Yuval-Davis, 2006, p 209). These elements indicate that the scope of belonging is much wider than formal legal citizenship.

Nira Yuval-Davis (2006) draws a distinction between 'belonging' and 'the politics of belonging' that is relevant for understanding the citizenship stories of the applicants. She identifies belonging primarily as emotional attachment, feeling 'at home' and feeling safe, whereas the politics of belonging is about inclusion or exclusion of people in terms of membership (Yuval-Davis, 2006, p 197). Citizenship applicants deal with both aspects in their accounts in this book. Scholars, however, are usually more interested in the politics of belonging than trying to gauge belonging itself as an emotive component of the migrant experience.

By contrast, belonging matters to citizenship applicants in all its aspects, particularly its emotive dimensions. The word 'belong' comes

up frequently when people narrate their citizenship experiences (55 times in 30 transcripts, 'belonging' is used more rarely (10 times). But word usage is less important than the context in which these words come up and their associated meanings. For example, a long-term resident from Greece says on an online immigration forum:

> I may not have a British passport or citizenship, but I feel quite British (even though I cook my own meals). I pay my taxes here, read British newspapers and novels, worry about issues in the UK and speak in English far more than I do in Greek. I even started drinking beer here, which I rarely touched in Greece.[14]

Here the words 'belong' or 'belonging' are not used, but the words 'feel quite British' indicate a sense of comfort that is crucial to belonging in a place.

As with James, legal status is not determinative of a feeling of belonging to Britain or identifying as British. People can have a strong sense of belonging without having legal status. But there is a link between feelings of belonging and claiming the right to stay and to work in a place (Ervine and Ervine, 2008). Monica Weiler Varsanyi (2005) finds that those who have a sense of belonging are more likely to apply for resident permits and proceed to full citizenship. Yet, there may be many other reasons for applying for citizenship, such as pragmatic needs. Basic passport holding is of critical importance to many (if not nearly all) applicants.

On the other hand, having legal status does not mean there is automatically an associated sense of belonging. Mani, the engineer who eventually obtained citizenship, said:

"Why would I feel British when I had to do what I did to continue working in this country? I needed the passport and it was a struggle. At no point I felt accepted or was made welcome. I am glad to be here but that is not related to feeling I am from here."

Shaheeda, who was born in Pakistan and has lived nearly 10 years in Lincoln, described her feelings on the subject:

"It is hard to say one is from England when people here don't treat you like that. If they could treat me as one of them, I would be one of them. Having passport does not make me one. English people are very nice to me but more like with guest. Very polite. I don't think I will ever say I am from here. I may be citizen but still feel like guest."

Further, legal status is also an ambiguous concept because immigration trajectories can meander between legality and illegality. Applicants do not always understand their legal situation well and are often uncertain of the implications of their immigration track records. For instance, in an immigration law online discussion forum, a user 'robbie2g2', who is a naturalisation applicant, posted the following comment in July 2016:

> I have been rejected on the basis that I had been illegal in the country prior to getting my refugee status and for working illegally in the country prior to applying for asylum. In short, I came into the country in 2002 as a student on a student visa which I stuck to its conditions mainly on the allowed working hours for students (that is 20hrs a week during term time and more during study holidays.). This I maintained up until 2007 and kept renewing. In 2007, I then applied for asylum and was registered as an asylum seeker until late 2008 where I was granted refugee status.
>
> I have progressed since then and now hold indefinite leave to remain. Recently my naturalisation got declined due to the fact that I was here illegally whilst I was an asylum seeker and on top of that I have been penalised for working whilst I held the student visa. I am lost for words as I believe when one is an asylum seeker, they are not necessarily illegal (I stand corrected) and that on a student visa I was allowed to work 20hrs a week and more only on holidays which I stuck to. So, believe I haven't broken any laws.

This user does not understand why the pre-ILR requirements led to the eventual refusal of his application for citizenship. Many applicants for refugee status who shared their stories in events or in online boards were similarly uncertain of whether their ILR status was sufficient or whether they had to proceed to citizenship as a legal requirement. The reasoning behind use of discretion at every stage remained unfathomable to many applicants. Similarly, children and young people born outside the UK often wrongly believe they hold British citizenship when, in law, they are not always British.

Belonging and the politics of belonging

John Crowley (1999) and Nira Yuval-Davis (2011) have differentiated belonging from the politics of belonging. The politics of belonging is about boundary maintenance dividing populations into 'us' and 'them'. It feeds into a formal structure of membership that is an official, state-held vision, but this vision permeates perceptions held by the general population. Membership (of a group) and ownership (of a place) are the key factors in any politics of belonging (Crowley, 1999, p 25). Belonging is an intimate, personal feeling (Fenster, 2005).

The politics of belonging has an impact on personal sense of belonging when it excludes someone. This exclusion may be completely unintentional. Abbas's story shows how exclusion can even be well meaning in nature. Abbas migrated as a young man from Iran to settle in a small English town in the South West. He felt isolated in a largely white town and continued to feel isolated after getting his British passport and acquiring a 'British accent'. He said he felt 'exotic':

"Everyone would speak of any Asian country they knew to me. Everything I did was related to some country, some place I did not know. Like food from India! It was hard until I had a girlfriend who was born and brought up here. She's English and her family took me in … like a stray. I remember the time we all supported Andy Murray in his first Wimbledon win and everyone forgot my origins. We yelled together and whooped with joy. I think I felt suddenly like I was one of them. Here with my girl, her brothers, their pals. It was so nice. I've had a passport for ages. But who cares? You don't have citizenship scrawled on your forehead…. So I'm kind of like – everything is mixed up, and so you don't feel a sense of belonging, because just having a passport or citizenship doesn't mean that you belong to a community or to a society or to a city. People can make you feel you are always outsider even when they are being kind, you know. They don't mean anything bad. Well sometimes they do … most often they are trying to bond by showing they know Iran is somewhere in Asia or at least they know Pakistan or India or something else exotic! But it alienates, made me feel strange."

For Abbas, the visual image of citizenship is one of the Wimbledon tennis championships. The connection is not that he plays tennis or has ever attended matches but the memory of his feeling of belonging in his girlfriend's family during the tournament that summer of 2013.

Length of residence and security

The most relevant factor for developing a sense of belonging is time itself. People and places matter in narrations of belonging, but time matters more. People construct belonging through interactions and this takes place over time as they become more acquainted with their new country. Bill, an economics professor of American origin living in London, recounted:

"Yes, I noticed in recent years that I made a switch from my teaching, where I stopped talking about the students as 'You', when I'm talking about them as British people and I would say 'We', or 'In our country' or something like that. I didn't mean to suggest that I was British in some formal sense but that – I made that switch when it was sounding funny to me that I would say, 'You', and so I would be excluding myself in that sense. It was like I do live here and I do know – it was the same thing, it was the shared recent past, you know?... So, talking about, 'Remember when we had the Jubilee a couple of years –' so I can't say, 'When you had the Jubilee', right? That sounds weird to me. Whereas when I first arrived here it wouldn't have felt like my Jubilee, it would have felt like theirs."

Length of residence also reinforces a sense of security for people and leads to the consolidation of legal rights such as through establishing ILR (for non-EEA nationals) or permanent residence (EEA nationals). Obtaining a secure legal status could consolidate belonging; thus Fenster (2005) calls the law a 'formal structure of belonging'. For example, holding an ILR permit allows for a change of employer, so, for workers, obtaining ILR is a very important step towards stability.

Legal status is an important precondition of participation. Legal status and the attendant right to participate fully in society contributes to the development of a sense of real belonging (Mee, 2009, p 844). Conversely, without status one is invisible in society, so it is hard for an individual to develop a sense of place-belongingness under those conditions. Applicants mention loneliness and isolation, as well as other kinds of mental health problems, in relation to when they did not feel that they belonged in their local neighbourhood and could not participate wholly at work. Madhu, resident of South London who originally came to the UK on a dependants' visa from India, describes how exit and entry into the country and not knowing anybody in her neighbourhood caused her deep distress:

> "I have more advanced degrees than my husband and when I came to join him here in England they asked me questions like, 'Are you just coming to join him or simply to look for a job?'. Now, my dependant visa allows me to work so what is the problem if I look for a job? Anyway, I told them I am coming to join him. But it made me feel so uneasy. Since then I had to travel to conferences in other countries and each time I was nervous coming back in. I always felt I could be stopped. With my dependant visa, I was asked so many questions in other European countries too, in Germany for instance, the guy wanted to see my address proof in UK. It was about not being from the EU as well. I was living in a very quiet place, modern builds where no one knew me. My husband knew people from work and I knew no one and struggled to find anyone to speak to. I would walk in the park and sometimes see if I could at least say hello to someone. It was a pretty awful time until I found work. I needed it to just be able to talk to someone. I can't imagine how I survived those days."

It is not surprising, then, that gaining security of status is the most common reason that applicants give for opting for citizenship. Psychological well-being appears individual in nature and internal to one's mind, but it is really about seeking recognition and acceptance from others and about being able to exist in a stable manner in society. Karim, who gained refugee status prior to opting for citizenship, reported feeling vulnerable as a refugee and regaining a sense of self as a citizen:

> "I was a professional, a father, a brother, a son. Then suddenly I was nothing but refugee in England. Refugees have no choice but we feel somehow in the wrong. I was ashamed of being nothing but refugee. Now I am a citizen, a father, a professional

again. I can make jokes, play football with my mates in the park, take my son to school without looking ashamed. I work and feel being citizen has made it all possible. It is not charity now for me."

The notion of safety and security was repeatedly mentioned by research participants as a rationale for seeking citizenship. Veena is a woman whose family came to the UK in the 1970s when the Ugandan government asked all Asians to leave (see Chapter One for the background to the *East African Asians* case). Veena was a little child at that time and she recalls the struggles of her parents and her uncle to enter and live in the UK (initially in Leicester and then in Bristol) and then to gain legal status here. She also remembers she felt safe in England, happy to have got away from the racial tension in Uganda:

"I missed my toys. I had these dolls I would teach in pretend play. Each one had a name and I still remember each one of the dolls by name and face. I had a blackboard. I would do them little report cards. I had to leave all of those behind when we came here. We could carry nothing. I am British of course ... but I know the British government was not welcoming at all to my parents and we felt very let down for years. We were not refugees. We had British passports and yet we were made to feel like refugees and soon we started feeling like ones. Bristol was harder for us as Leicester already had many Asians but we were amongst first few in Bristol.... But as an adult I have gone back many times to Uganda and I go back now as a British woman. Uganda of my childhood is just in my head. It does not exist any more."

Safety from gender discrimination was a point made by migrant–citizens from South Asia and parts of Africa. Sarla, a woman who grew up in a large city in India (a city she did not want named in the book), struggled with the immigration and citizenship journey as she (desperately) did not want to return to 'a culture of violence'. In her own words:

> "I grew up always fearing rape and sexual harassment. It is not that it does not happen in Manchester. But that daily fear of being felt up in public transport or having a man follow you down streets or making lewd comments out in open ... even as a child you learn to fear that. I was always secondary to every man and I could not accept it. I got freedom when I came to England. I was not secondary any more. I could dream of being someone. That is why I love this country. I came as an economic migrant but I am actually a refugee from the daily violence faced by women in many large Indian cities."

There were a number of interviewees and storytellers who sought citizenship to consolidate their children's family ties and sense of belonging in Britain rather than their own. Jan, who was born in Poland, has two British-born (registered as British) children. He decided to apply for his own citizenship once his children moved from primary school to secondary school in Glasgow:

> "They [the children] strongly identify as Scottish. They live here and I do not see any reason to ever move back to Poland. I do visit my town there every year to see my relatives there but there was no point in not being British. My children started worrying when there were initial discussions on Brexit [the UK's withdrawal from the European Union] and I was not going to let them feel different from their friends. I went to my lawyer in the very early days and got it all sorted as quickly as I could."

Englishness and Britishness

Not every migrant–citizen discusses belonging in the UK in terms of freedom from fear or persecution. Many choose to become citizens for practical convenience: passport and travel come top of the list of reasons for seeking citizenship. Another fear that propels applications is that the rules will change and become stricter with time, so, in order to avoid these moving goalposts, people often proceed sooner than they otherwise might. Further, belonging is a multifaceted concept that can signify territorial connections or relational ones. Ann Dummett and Andrew Nicol (1990, p 53) write in their seminal work on British nationality and immigration, *Subjects, citizens, aliens and others*: 'There is no historical consistency about Britishness, nor even geographical certainty'.

References to national belonging come about in myriad ways in stories. Dummett and Nicol (1990, p 21) point out that the UK has a connection with territory rather than any ethnic people, unlike Germany, which is a nation connected to its people. Migrant–citizens often refer to Britishness but mean it in a variety of ways: belonging to the UK, belonging to Wales, belonging to/in Scotland, being Scottish, being Welsh, being British, and being English.

While Britishness is the most common reference point, storytellers are also wary of 'British values' being exclusionary values. Despite this wariness, people often identify certain characteristics as 'British' and then include themselves as holding these very same values. Examples of British values that narrators use to include themselves as British are: tea drinking; love for the Queen; strawberries and cream at Wimbledon (the tennis in general); cricket; loving dogs; pub quizzes; the BBC and television shows; street parties; politeness and respect for rules; beer; and, in one instance, surreal comedy (Monty Python). These are everyday idioms that people use to capture the meaning of nationhood for them (Fox and Miller-Idriss, 2008).

Migrant–citizens warm up to more specific regional references such as being Welsh or Scottish when they speak of acquiring these identities. Dummett and Nicol (1990, p 22) note that English common law has influenced understandings of Britishness. However, Englishness as an identity is not one that migrant–citizens are comfortable with in their stories. For many, being English is more racialised than being British or being Welsh. Englishness, more than any other national identity within the UK, ties in closely with being white or being colonisers (albeit in historical times). Sometimes, the storytellers conflate Britishness and Englishness in an unreflective manner while discussing belonging, but, even then, this appears to take place mostly in the context of negative experiences. Robbie Shilliam (2016, p 244) writes that 'Englishness, a culture of belonging that owed much to the white Diaspora for its development, was racially exclusive for the most part'.

Jürgen Habermas (1994), while formulating a procedural model of citizenship, has argued that citizenship is not tied to any ethnic identity. It is not as much as about who one is, as about what one does. Similarly, Seyla Benhabib (2002) says that citizenship is social practice rather than identity or legality. However, the data analysed in this book indicates that through social practice people can establish a sense of belonging that then helps imbibe particular identities. Their sense of belonging is affected, however, whenever they are repeatedly asked to re-establish their 'Britishness'. Ethnic minority citizens resent proving again and again that they are 'British enough' as law and legal process often demand through presence for number of days and language and knowledge tests. In the words of a South African origin participant at a storytelling event:

"One thing that interests me is the hoops that we have to jump through to be accepted, and the whole concept of Britishness, and how – whether people actually acquire that, especially if you consider skin colour, perhaps, and extending beyond that, people who constantly have their Britishness questioned, and that can be no matter how high up you get within the system, whether you're doing really well for yourself, just to have someone say, 'Go back where you come from', is something that is that stark reminder … the constant need to prove your Britishness, or to prove that you belong here …"

Another participant had family who migrated to the US from Ireland in the 1960s. She was born in the US in the 1970s, but, in her turn, migrated to England. She said:

"As migrants turning into citizens there is this need to establish extra loyalty … so I find myself talking of family members who took part in the war effort, or some award of some sort … highlighting achievements…. That is totally unnecessary for someone who has lived generations on this soil. But we have to do that."

The extra loyalty appears to be a price for holding multiple identities. As another participant put it: "How to be both British and Muslim. Or British and another citizenship holder. These things create personal challenges. A need to be extra good at all times to prove you are not bad".

Colonial citizenship and colonial belonging

An interesting kind of belonging in the British context is belonging related to colonial connections, such as imperial subjecthood and the subsequent Commonwealth connection. One storytelling event participant, Akasi, explained how her grandfathers identified as British in Ghana but how her own self-identification as British (growing up in England) is quite different from the post-colonial sense of belonging of her grandparents:

"After independence it's sort of weird the way in which they felt British, and because I grew up in the UK there was a disconnect between their Britishness and my Britishness. Their Britishness was acquired. Neither of my grandfathers came to the UK, but they felt British because they had been told they were British, and they had to pay taxes to the British, and everything was — well, one of my grandfathers had a very huge, massive cocoa farm, so they had to send most of their cocoa to the UK. So, they felt British because that was everything in their lives was British. The work they did went to the UK."

Akasi spoke of how deeply entrenched the Britishness was in a humorous account of her grandfather who lived until he was 107:

"… when he felt he was going to die, this was when he was about 99 so he felt he may die soon, he told us that if it happened that he died that we should keep him in the mortuary for a while, write a letter to the Queen, and let the Queen know that he had gone [laughs]. So, he didn't say, 'Let the president of Ghana know'. He said, 'Write to the Queen and let her know that I have finally died' … [laughs]."

Another applicant from Somalia was brought to the UK as a young child because her father decided there is a deep existing connection between Somalia and Britain:

"My dad, he's just got this sense of right to be in the UK; not to opt to be Dutch. Some of my sisters and family stayed in Holland, because they were older and they had a choice, legally, to say, 'We're staying', but I was younger so I had to come with my dad to England. But he was like, 'No, we belong here in England, because we were colonised by the British. The British were in our lands, they were in our country. We worked together', he said this in a positive way, not in a negative slavery way, because historically, I think Somalis were never slaves.… But for me, a young black female in the UK, for me colonisation: wow, that's negative."

She narrated her experiences of racism in her childhood in a small, northern English town and how disappointed she was about this as she had not expected anything of that nature after hearing her father's positive depiction of England.

Paul, from the Caribbean islands, said he felt British well before his arrival because the small island nation of his birth "is part of the Commonwealth, the Queen's head is on currency, the formal education system is British". Another participant, from India, recalled:

"I grew up on a diet of Enid Blyton books and as a sickly child had more books than friends for company. I was in love with the English countryside before I ever set eyes on England. I also loved Ireland as I attended Irish catholic school. Strangely to me Ireland and England were one in my childhood. Something I am embarrassed about now. But in Calcutta of my childhood the two were rolled into one. When I first visited England, I was still a child and very familiar with everything from books. Later as I returned as an adult, it was as if I had never been away. By then I had lived nearly eight years in the US and there everyone found my 'British' accent 'cute' so I guess I was somehow identified as British. I am not sure what they meant by British though!"

Similarly, a connection through colonial relations is present in this story of an American applicant whose ancestors had migrated from Scotland:

"Well, if I just may say that through my experience, and also people from communities that I'm from, that colonisation has a big part in feeling a sense of belonging in Britain, for example. So, I have, for example, my parents would say, 'Your great grandfather was buried here, because through colonisation he was a seaman and he travelled to Britain, and that city is where he passed away'. So, my family felt already a sense of belonging – you know? And some of us came through parts of different European countries, and ended up, again, in England, because of that connection through colonisation. Migration is not just one way. It can be quite circular!"

Colonisation, while abhorred by most applicants from former colonial nations, has significant legal effects (as seen in the *East African Asians* case discussed in Chapter One), for example, providing a route to former colonials whose grandparents were born in the UK to seek an ancestry visa. This route is mostly restricted to ethnically white people because non-white ancestors were unlikely to have been born within the territorial limits of the UK. One storyteller from Australia reflects on this colonial relationship, which privileges white people. Jean is now an indefinite leave-holder thanks to her UK ancestry visa and she is now almost a British citizen. She says:

"My grandfather actually fought for the allies in Germany, for four years. It used to really anger me when I used to come into the UK and have to wait in the non-EEA line to go through customs, or go through immigration, and it used to really anger me where I was thinking about him and that I had to stand in this line and that I couldn't just go through. I felt that I had an entitlement, almost, to come in. Then I've been reflecting on that a lot more as I've gone through the process, which has been very easy for me, actually. So, I get to stay for five years with a UK ancestry visa, which I wouldn't have been entitled to, but for being white, and then once the five years rolls around, I just get the indefinite leave to remain. I paid the money, or my employer paid the money. It was a lot of money. Anyway, I just get it automatically. So, I've reflected on, I think, my position of privilege in respect of how that process has gone and how easy it's been for me, and also because I'm classed as white, and I've got this kind of colonial accent which there's quite a lot of tolerance for, I think, in the UK, as opposed to other accents, so I haven't really experienced any kind of direct discrimination or anything. So that's been quite easy for me, and I think that's a reflection of my position of privilege as I approached this process."

Urban and rural place-belongingness

Colonisation is related to territorial conquest, but territory also plays a strong role in the imaginations of people about belonging. While national identity can be experienced locally, and the immediate spatial surroundings can have a direct impact on people's lives, national belonging is often a more abstract concept. The global city is the cradle of migration and migrant–citizens are able to make connections in cities. The data from migrant–citizen stories indicates that there is a tremendous difference between urban and suburban or rural locations. There follow some examples of stories that highlight the differences in migrant experiences.

One social worker, who migrated from Somalia, works with asylum seekers located all over the country. She said:

> "… national belonging is completely different, but city belonging for people is much easier, because of the diversity of cities, and just having a sense of belonging to a city is usually a lot stronger for long-term migrants or people who are in the city neighbourhood and they have their favourite places to go, to bring friends to hang out with in the city, but may not identify with the nation status as such, or feeling of nationally belonging."

Another migrant–citizen from Sierra Leone, who grew up in the countryside in the Midlands, explains how her aunt never liked visiting her:

> "… my aunt left Sierra Leone to come to Britain, and basically, she first came to Bristol, and she felt really welcomed by everyone here, which is amazing. But whenever she would come and visit me and my family, who live in quite a rural village, it was just totally different. I know this is slightly more on the topic of racism, rather than citizenship, but I just think the divide and the differences between urban and rural places is just so huge."

Metin, who had lived for 16 years in suburban Germany, then settled down in London and became a British citizen, said he could not settle in Germany because he "stuck out in the white, German neighbourhood". He found London easy to live in and explained this as follows:

> "So it's something positive in London that's happening, it is global. I feel like a sense of belonging here in London, because

London has got such a positive look on immigration and citizenship, and status, and everyone feels the belonging here. I have a Turkish shop in my corner. Polish friends to hang out with. English friends at work. So, bit of everything. People like it. It makes London exciting."

Many migrant–citizens echoed Metin's words and emphasised belonging to a particular city rather than to the country. A city identity appears to coexist more easily with any previous or simultaneous foreign nationality they hold. As Vanessa (who arrived from Kenya) said:

"I can be Londoner and still be from Kenya when I visit family. There people will not like hearing of my Britishness, although I feel so British … easier to talk about London without letting down a poorer country. There are many people who appear to be snobs: becoming wealthy Africans in Europe. I don't want to be one of those people. People understand London as a city for people from all over the world. They do not mind my being Londoner."

Cities are not just about scale or monolithic blocks for migrants. At a storytelling event, Hasan from Egypt says that the entire city consists of a number of villages. There are favourite grocery stores, street corners, even bus stops where one sees the same characters every day, and these become a familiar presence over time for migrants. Strong local attachments can be formed if the locality embraces cosmopolitan values. But, Hasan pointed out, a city is not always uniformly welcoming to migrants. There are pockets of greater diversity where migrants develop a sense of the local in the global, and there are other parts that are usually quite forbidding for ethnic minorities. He said:

"Things are probably different for European migrants. They would not have the Harrods shop chaps following them if they entered there or Apple store guys concerned if they are there to just waste time. These things have happened to me. I have a good job, I dress well, live in London. But still ..."

These negative experiences challenge people's sense of belonging, but some migrant–citizens are nonchalant about negative local experiences:

"I expect certain amount of racism. I know that sounds terrible. But it is like sexual violence. It does not happen always, but as a woman you know it might if you are around the wrong person. So as a black woman I just learned to expect both sometimes when around wrong people. It is not nice ... it does not stay uppermost on my mind all the time. It is under the surface a lot of times."

Race appears to be a predominant idea in less diverse areas, as one participant eloquently put it: "Growing up in a small village I was called so many names in school. I was just one of three non-white kids in school. It was terrible for me".

Relational aspects of belonging

Strong and weak ties

Territorial belonging is only one critical dimension of belonging. The other important aspect is the relational one, which is about connections people make in their community. Territorial and relational belonging are very closely connected. The long-term presence of family members and close friends helps develop territorial belonging, as does creating new relationships of love and friendship. Sometimes, newer migrants do not have any ancestral connections to a land, so they develop strong connections through more recent attachments. If significant others are not there, casual everyday encounters generally do not support strong feelings of belonging. However, the weak links created by casual meetings and conversations (at the corner shop or in parks) help such people to survive acute loneliness in the period during which they have not yet established stronger ties.

Having several strong connections gives one a sense of rootedness. One story about food and its centrality in making connections in community organisations is pertinent. Sonia, who is originally from India and holds British partiality (which entitles her to live in the UK without any restriction), said:

> "I'm very involved with my church here, very involved with my school community, so I feel … I can bake. I bake and cook – I'm doing afternoon sandwiches for a friend this afternoon and fruit, or I can bake cakes or I do a good roast – I love roast pork and apple sauce and I love a good curry. I think I would say that I'm really equally comfortable – when I'm in India, I can integrate; when I'm in England, I utterly integrate into English ways and English life and have a lot of very dear English friends. Being a good cook helps!"

The workplace

A critical aspect in developing relational belonging is the importance of work and the workplace. The following story, 'The shoemaker and the shoes', is based on the experiences of an EEA national from France, Catherine, who is now British. Catherine is a lawyer who came to England with her scientist husband. She did not have a job on arrival. She had children in the UK (four in the space of 10 years) and finished a Master's degree while constantly looking for suitable employment. She was unable to find a job in any law firm and then, quite by chance, while working as a volunteer, she was asked to assist with immigration advice in a law centre. From thereon she became a regular adviser on immigration advice, qualified as a solicitor, and started working full time. She felt that, until she had full-time work, she had never quite belonged in the UK. Without a job, and without citizenship, she was always an EEA national waiting to return some day to France. For Catherine, work opened up friendships in a way motherhood could not:

"It was so fulfilling to have skills that were needed and it seems so strange that it all happened quite by accident. Had I not met one woman from the law centre, and she just asked me to help out, my career would not have taken off."

Ironically, once Catherine started working in immigration law practice, she was constantly helping other EEA nationals apply for British citizenship. She had delayed her own application for British citizenship mostly because she had been too busy as a mother and then as a lawyer to fill in her application. It is at this point in the story that she remarked:

"I was the shoemaker who did not have a pair of shoes for herself. You see what I mean, there I was explaining to all my clients how valuable it was to get British citizenship. How they should apply. And myself, I did not have time to apply! One day a friend said, 'Catherine, how come you are not a citizen?'. I was bit stunned. I had been so busy I did not even think about it. Now I laugh when I look back. Anyway, it was then I got all my documents together and put in the application. Thank God, I did it then, can you imagine now? With all the confusion of Brexit? Now clients have to get permanent residence card first, fill huge form. I have a surge in work from EEA applicant clients these days. Everybody who has lived for years, now wants to suddenly get to vote and make a difference. I am tempted to ask them why they did not bother all this time, but then I delayed so long myself, I can't ask others that question. I understand that we did not feel the pinch, us from Europe, so we got complacent."

EEA nationals and ties

Catherine's point about EEA nationals not feeling the 'pinch' is a valid one. Until the Brexit vote, EEA nationals were treated the same as British citizens as long as they were workers (not retired nationals moving post-retirement or students). This is still the case at the time of writing, but the expectation is that there will soon be changes to the rights of EEA nationals in the UK. Until now, family members of EEA nationals have had better rights than British citizens as they could come and join their EEA partners without any requirement to prove a minimum income. Spouses and children of British citizens can only join them if the family meets threshold minimum income requirements (Guild, 2016, p 58).

Why have EEA nationals been protected in this manner, thereby (in Catherine's words) "lulling them into a false sense of security"? Ackers and Dwyer (2004) write that European Union (EU) citizenship developed from its embryonic stages in the 1950s to be formally constituted by the Treaty on European Union of 1993. It requires member states to deliver social rights to qualifying EU nationals who migrate. There is great divergence in standards of social welfare delivery across the region, but the provision is non-discriminatory between nationals of a member country and other EU citizens present there. The model is imperfect, as it is mostly based on the needs of a male migrant worker who takes his family with him. Those who move following retirement (and have never worked outside their 'home' country) arguably do not gain anything much from this model of EU citizenship. Families (imagined as mostly female dependants and children) are treated as fixed legal categories, rather than being dynamic ones that change over time. Nevertheless, the principles of free movement and non-discrimination mean that worker EEA nationals have been able to claim, by and large, similar legal rights to their British counterparts in Britain.

EEA nationals who are long-term residents in the UK have also had greater access to 'cultural capital' than many other migrant–citizens from around the world. Like Erel (2010), who applies a Bourdieusian concept of cultural capital to how migrants seek work and use networks, it is possible to see how being European confers distinct advantages to long-term residents. Languages such as French and German are in demand in the UK, so Catherine could support herself as a French language tutor for several years. EEA nationals have more professional friends, as most EEA migrants move freely for work (by design of the treaty) and the distance between home countries and host countries is not great compared with other parts of the world (Ryan and Mulholland, 2014). These networks help in getting jobs and then developing feelings of belonging because strong ties develop through work. The absence of a colonial legacy and associated racism also assist in feelings of rootedness in the UK.

Paradoxically, as Catherine mentioned, EEA nationals could gainfully be part of skilled employment in the UK without seeking citizenship or even settled status. Therefore, there has been little to incentivise them to formally seek British citizenship. With the threat of Brexit looming over them, and daily media accounts of rejections of permanent residence applications of EEA nationals, EEA nationals who have lived in the UK for long periods have started applying for British citizenship. There is a deep sense of hurt and betrayal at the sudden turn of events after the referendum held on 23 June 2016. The three million EEA nationals in the UK have strong organising voices in campaign groups such as The 3 Million. Despite repeated reassurances by politicians, it remains to be seen whether EEA nationals will be able to retain secure statuses in the UK in the post-Brexit era. Meanwhile, their current situation is a cautionary tale of what happens when supra-national membership crumbles.

Multiple belonging

Long-term residents, whether EEA nationals or other kinds of nationals, seldom have loyalty only to one place and one set of people. Belonging for long-term residents is usually complex and capable of being expressed as simultaneous loyalty (Waite and Cook, 2011). Some EEA nationals (for example, those from the Netherlands) and residents of other countries where dual nationality is not permitted (for instance, India) are reluctant to lose the nationality of their country of origin by becoming British. This could be for pragmatic reasons, such as inability to buy property as a foreigner in the other country (India, for example, places restrictions on foreign nationals in this regard), or affective ones (not wanting to lose the sense of close connection to relations in the country of birth). This does not translate into disloyalty of any sort, but is a natural effect of accumulated human memories and identity over time. As one participant mentioned: "People do not start as blank pages in new places". Mihir, of Indian national origin, said in an online immigration forum:

> I would have liked to have kept my Indian citizenship if it was possible. I feel Indian but I feel British, too. This is a duality. UK is my main home, India is my former home.[15]

Many migrants are grateful they can hold dual nationalities and cite the ability to hold another additional nationality as a reason for why they opted for British citizenship. Migrants who maintain links with their former/other nationality countries often resent the suspicion with which they are viewed in the UK. For example, storytelling participant Sarla says:

"I do not need to prove I love this country more by forsaking the other one. I am here in the present and am contributing here. But I have old parents whose health I have to think of. I need to be able to still go over and run things there [India] sometimes. Why make people choose? It reminds me of the time a stupid politician said choose English cricket team over Indian or Pakistani one. It is ridiculous. I love this country because I choose to be here. If you are just born here, you are the one who should have to show you truly love being here. You are a mere accident of birth. I took decisions that brought me here. Making naturalised or dual nationals prove loyalty is playground behaviour."

Letting go of belonging

The holding of multiple identities is not just a fertile ground for external suspicions; it can also create inner turmoil. Alina's story is illustrative of this conflict.

"Citizenship paperwork did not mean anything for me in terms of being or feeling British, if anything it was a pain getting to the point of holding a passport. I felt British long before. Not sure exactly when. But it just happened. Home here replaced home in Kuala Lumpur, though I can't ever tell that to my parents. They'll be sad ... I realised how I did not miss my old life strangely when I lost this torn, brown diary I had from 1992. The diary had so many names and addresses from way back ... people I met in school, relatives of relatives, old neighbours and friends. People all in Malaysia from long back. A few who had migrated too. Someone in Australia was mentioned to me as a

'contact' as they had left Malaysia and would know about life 'outside' [chuckles]. So, he was in the diary too. Never contacted him but who knows, might have some day. The diary has moved with my other papers and stuff from house to house in London. I took care of it. But then one day I lost it. I think I left it on a bus while looking for a book to read. Can't be sure as did not miss it for a while. At first, I searched everywhere and cried my eyes out. I did not have those numbers or addresses anywhere else. Then a strange thing happened … I started feeling free. Free of my life in Malaysia, of those people who really did not mean anything to me.... Not sure why I felt this way. By then my real life was in London. The women I was friends with from when I had my babies were in London. We had bonded over birthing classes in the Royal London Hospital. Stayed in touch with toddlers and then school-going kids. We had shared much more than anyone I grew up with. One of them even came for my citizenship ceremony. Same at work. Girls who covered for me, and whom I covered for, when in need. And, we all come from somewhere else. Ukraine, New Zealand, Scotland. But all Londoners. I guess, I had moved on long back but did not like to admit it. So, losing the diary really set me free. I could be British, be Londoner, be me."

Alina's story was told with some humour, but her narrative also demonstrates her anxiety about letting go of the past as it felt like betraying her parents and self-identifying as a 'Londoner'. She used the loss of the diary to disclose a lot about the development of new relationships in the community (through friendship at work and through being a new mother in London). This transition had happened over the years in an organic and non-reflective manner. She described at length how she had moved house several times but kept the diary and the contacts in it carefully, fully expecting to be in touch with all these people throughout life. There were several idealised memories attached to the names and addresses. Yet, she now felt released from the weight of these memories. Alina started out talking about her citizenship application and how one of her uncles had provided her with contact details of a law firm in London that could potentially help her. That led her to discuss other relations and friends who had migrated and then to mention the diary, which contained several names of importance. At this point, she veered off course from her citizenship story to the story of the loss of the diary. Clearly, this loss, which happened around the same time as her application, had marked the closing of a chapter in her life, and she associated it with the new sense of rootedness she felt. She went on to discuss what the citizenship process meant to her, and emphasised that change in legal status did not provide her with a greater sense of belonging:

"It was not something that was just the one event when they make you citizen. It is knowing you live here permanently and you have friends here who accept you. My children made me feel British much before any ceremony because I had to quickly learn about it all. They are very British, being in school, and it is nice. It helped me too. But yes, getting the paperwork was a special feeling too. It was emotional. But not making me feel more British, I already felt British being a working Londoner mum."

Alina has chosen, to some extent, to let go of her Malaysian identity. She did this through a process of internal reflection and was not pressured in any manner to 'become British'.

A similar story is of dual national Bill (both an American and British citizen), who explained how, with time, his political sense of duty led him to British citizenship:

"… in the US on a day-to-day level, I don't follow things closely, I'm not particularly well informed and so I don't think that it's right to vote. But if you invert that logic, then I can tick all those boxes here, and so I feel like I can and do have a moral duty to contribute to the political process in some way in the UK. So, that was something that happened about the time of the elections last year and then it just became, is sort of a time issue. The application is not as bad as it looks but it's just, you go [mimics sighing] 'Oh, when am I going to do this? I don't want to do this this evening; I don't want to do it on the weekend. When am I going to do this? It's just a kind of pain in the ass'. But I ended up doing it at some point just because it got to that point. That point where I just had to express my British political views and was not bothered enough to follow American ones any more."

As in Alina's account, there is also the conflict of choice making in Bill's life. He has let go of some of the depth of feeling for his former home and made his full commitment to his current one from an internal sense of obligation. The internal obligation is directly related to feelings of belonging, rather than to any external censure or approbation.

Choice and expectations

Elspeth Probyn (1996, p 5) defines belonging as 'a desire for becoming other', a longing to be with someone, or to be something else. This makes belonging a process (of becoming) rather than a status (of being). Belonging is very similar to Habermasian procedural citizenship (Habermas, 1992). When migrants choose to become someone new by breaking free of their past, they find emotional belonging easier. For instance, women who seek greater personal freedom than available in more conservative societies find it easier to 'feel' British than those who would like to carry on the traditions of their home countries in an orthodox manner. However, not all migrant–citizens are seeking to reinvent themselves. Those who become British for economic reasons generally proactively bring their past into their present lives. Herein, the politics of belonging comes into play if they are unable to continue past practices for structural reasons. Should they face barriers in carrying out religious or cultural practices simply for being too different from majoritarian society, they are likely to experience lack of belonging and even alienation.

The rhetoric of sameness, which clearly prevents any recognition of difference, contributes to alienation. Forced assimilation to the language, culture, values, behaviour and religion of the dominant group can result in a backlash from minorities who experience domination (Yuval-Davis, 2006, p 209). Further, even if willing migrant–citizens like Alina or Bill choose to adopt the dominant culture and practices, it is likely that their accents, skin colour or unconscious behaviour would prevent full sameness and result in their exclusion from a complete sense of belonging.

Migrant–citizens also experience exclusion from their other cultures and their countries of origin. A migrant–citizen of Nigerian origin, Olufemi, said:

"Yes. If you flip that, so whenever I'm in Nigeria and I talk about stuff, they say, 'Well, go away from here, you're British', so again, it's a question of belonging, and like I said, the rules and this, it's not really just a British problem, it's a global problem."

Olufemi, while discussing her citizenship application, explained why there is a disconnect between legal formal citizenship and the emotions of belonging:

"They don't take into account how you feel about belonging. Everybody wants to belong somewhere. You tick that box, tick that box, tick that box and then you belong, it's completely unemotional, and I have been saying that a lot of what we see; an under-appreciation of emotion. Emotion is such a great part of who we are, and we then try to put that into boxes, and those boxes do not explain who we are, and I think that's part of the problem with bureaucracy."

The next chapter moves on to an examination of the theme of bureaucracy and belonging as it turns to the citizenship application process and its impact on belonging – Olufemi's words are a useful entry point for that discussion.

Conclusion

This chapter has drawn on the theme of 'belonging' from the life stories of long-term residents to illustrate what it means to them. Belonging is not just any one element of being in a particular location or in a community. It cannot be boxed into neat categories, but rather hinges on a range of interconnected relational positions with respect to places and people. As demonstrated through changing life situations, embodied experiences and memories of people, belonging for migrant–citizens goes far beyond territorial belonging and encompasses both the local and the global. Being situated in urban areas appears to facilitate both the local and the global identities that people possess, including diasporic links and the maintaining of distinct cultural identities. Time is also a major factor in how people view themselves in terms of their surrounding communities. Some people had inherited a sense of 'Britishness' from their parents or grandparents who had grown up in former colonial contexts or possessed a strong Commonwealth identity. Belonging and Britishness pervade people's sense of self even when they maintain multiple identities.

Issues of belonging go far beyond the legal process of gaining formal citizenship. Many of the stories recounted here have highlighted how people come to feel they are British long before naturalising, while stories in the next chapter show how naturalisation procedures sometimes chip away at 'Britishness'. Belonging is often questioned by applicants during the citizenship journey. The next two chapters concentrate on the impacts of the citizenship application process and legal procedures on belonging.

FOUR

Myths and legends: stories of struggles and disappointment

As the previous chapter demonstrated, stories of belonging are based on the micro-social experiences of people. These are subjective experiences of a wide variety, but nevertheless there are common trends that emerge from the data. While the storytellers in this book are all successful applicants, the data on citizenship application overwhelmingly establishes the process as a negative experience for most applicants. There is a disconnect between the legal process of acquiring citizenship and people's perceptions of Britishness and belonging in the UK. As Olufemi recounted in the previous chapter, the tick boxes of applications do not have space in them for 'belonging'. Thus, this chapter examines the challenges for long-term residents of becoming British citizens and then analyses the effect of these challenges on people's sense of belonging.

Expense and profit making

A challenge mentioned by everyone is the expense of the application process. Each part of the citizenship process costs money and the costs add up to large amounts. Many applicants try to save money by

completing the process themselves and not seeking legal help. Jane, of Canadian origin, mentioned: "After paying the required fees at each stage there is no spare money to go to a lawyer. I work two jobs and still could not afford it." Asim, a junior doctor based in Bristol, explained:

"The whole idea of citizenship is to someday for me to advance in the medical profession. Becoming a specialist. I am interested in paediatric care. But at time of applying I was struggling as a new medical student. How could I afford the process? I took on more debt just thinking I was improving my future chances but it was a difficult decision for me."

In a Scottish report on refugees who became citizens (Stewart and Mulvey, 2011, p 52), one participant stated:

I had to pay a lot of money, it's the most expensive thing I own, my British passport, I think, more expensive than any pair of shoes! What I did I waited a year from the time I got my indefinite status and then I had to apply for Naturalisation, well I waited more than a year because, to be honest, I couldn't afford it.

However, some applicants avoid delaying because they worry about future fee rises. At one storytelling event, Bill, a London-based economics professor of American origin, said: "The Home Office raises the fees all the time so if I did not do it now, my chances would worsen". Jan, of Polish origin, mentioned (tongue in cheek) that the expense was a bonding factor for migrants at citizenship ceremonies. He said:

"I did chat to the lady next to me, and we were asking one another how long we'd been in the UK, so I said over ten years, and she was in the UK for over 20 or something; a long time. And my question was like, 'So why did you apply now?' and I didn't say that my application today is before the fees grow by 25 per cent.... She looked at me and she was like, 'Oh, it's the fees, isn't it?'. I was like, 'Yes' [laughs]."

Akasi's partner (born in Ghana) has had to spend more and more money over the years applying for citizenship. The fees were only the starting point:

"Fees, I think now for an adult it's £1,300, but my partner, who got his citizenship last week, I think over the years he's probably spent something like four or five grands, in terms of the visas and top-up. He resents enriching the Home Office."

Even those who are confident about the application process worry about the fees because they fear that the Home Office will not refund anything, irrespective of the outcome of their case. Bill said:

"At my salary level it's not that – it wouldn't have been catastrophic but it would have been really upsetting to lose up to, what is it we paid, £2,500? More, with all the extra fees, the biometric enrolments, the nationality checking service, all these different things. I'm sure we paid £3,000 and to lose that, wow, that would be frustrating."

Georgina, born in Romania but now British and living in Wales, had submitted citizenship applications for her two children. She was appalled at having to pay extra money for their biometric enrolment. Worse followed when, after the biometric enrolment had been completed, she again got a reminder for both her children to be enrolled. She decided to ignore this letter, knowing that she had already completed that part of the process. A couple of weeks later, she got another letter, exactly the same as the first letter, but now addressed only to her daughter, that said: 'We need you to do your biometric enrolment'. She reflected:

"I thought, that's odd, we did it. Of course, the Post Office, they give you receipts of everything and whatnot. So, I thought, well, I should ring them and tell them that there's been a mistake, right? Then you go to the website to get the phone number, and there was a phone number that I had rung earlier, but the other phone number, it says you can only ring it if your application has been with us for at least six months, which it had not. So, I tried ringing the number anyhow and they did pick up the phone but all they said was I have to email the biometric email address or something like that. Which I then did, explaining the situation, sending PDFs of it and saying, if there was a problem with the biometric enrolment I'm happy to do it [smiles], I did not say 'happy' to do it again, I wasn't that British yet [smiles] – but I said I will do it again but please pay the fee for me so I can do it, because I'm not going to pay it a second time. There's no way that I made an error. So, I send that email and then about a week later we get a second letter, now it's for my son. This time it's not the carbon copy, it's actually a more specific letter that says his enrolment was not successful; we need you to do it again. But I still haven't had the email back from the first one. So, I send another email now saying, here's the receipts from his thing, saying please advise me how to do this. If you want me to do it, I'll do it but please pay the fee. I don't want to just keep coming back and paying £40 every time I come.

Of course, no response. I can't remember what happened next, I don't think I wrote to them again, but basically what ensued over the next two months, literally, were these emails. They would respond in about a two-week lag to one of my emails or something but in a very unhelpful and a very generic way, which would say something very short like, 'Yes, please do the biometric enrolment' and not responding to any of my queries and not really reading anything and not saying that there was a problem."

It was a complete mystery for Georgina why she was receiving these messages from the Home Office. It took her many weeks to sort out the situation and she eventually realised that the Home Office had mistakenly swapped her children's enrolment forms; her son's data was filed for her daughter's and vice versa. The fees aspect is what caused her most anxiety:

"It was the most infuriating thing because I could not keep paying. I would respond the same day to their response but then they would be responding a week later to a response that I had written a week before. You literally just felt like you were hitting your head against the wall, and you're paying incredibly premium prices for incredibly substandard service."

She elaborated:

"It took two months to figure this simple thing [the switch of her son's and daughter's applications] out and there was an email from them that said, 'Oh, you submitted the wrong application for' – you know. No, I didn't. I didn't submit anything. I took my children there, I know which one is my son, I know which one is my daughter, I can tell them apart. I do confuse their names sometimes but I didn't confuse them that day. I mean, it was just absolutely infuriating and I was getting so worked up about it, and then you get nervous because in the background there's this kind of £1,500 you've paid and is it going to be unsuccessful? You know that it won't be but it was frustrating."

Taking an interesting consumer viewpoint of the Home Office's services, she added:

"You think if you're paying £750 and there's no explanation anywhere about why you're paying these fees, you think you can expect service that matches the £750 fee. I think someone should be coming with tea and biscuits and saying. 'Oh, can I help you'; that's the level of service I expect for those prices. If I don't get that, I at least expect to be able to speak to someone, to clarify their mistake, right? Then I really did think that, many times, that I'm paying a hell of a lot of money for this and I deserve better service. The rationale behind charging the high fees was not made explicit on the website. I felt I should get better service."

Georgina survived the stress because she had colleagues of other nationalities who had also undergone the process and were part of her support network. Despite this, she had difficulty focusing on her work for very long, although she was lucky enough to have colleagues who often helped her manage her workload. The adverse effects of the stress inhibited any sense of being British, although, with time, she did not continue to feel alienated.

Mani, of Sri Lankan origin, recounts how paying an extra amount for expedited service got him nowhere. He waited six hours in the Croydon office of UK Visas and Immigration – a division of the Home Office – with his family (including young children) and was then sent away without a decision or refund for the hefty 'same-day service' fee. Years after this experience, Mani is still bitter about it.

Spending money in this manner is prohibitive for vast numbers of applicants. Writer Kamila Shamsie, who documented her own citizenship journey in a *Guardian* article,[16] said: 'The citizenship laws are, consequently, rapidly moving to the point where the only criteria for becoming British will be the size of your bank balance'. The idea of golden visas (Tier 1 visas) that are linked to investment capacity and lead to citizenship on a fast track is an example of the commercialisation of citizenship. Further, another recent *Guardian* article by Amelia Hill claims that there are profits of nearly 800 per cent on some visa applications.[17] A good example of the commodification of citizenship and its conceptualisation as property are the fees charged for children's citizenship. In a reply to a freedom of information request, the Home Office admitted overcharging for children's citizenship, but justified the profit making on grounds of the benefits individuals receive from holding citizenship.[18]

Documentation

Documentation requirements add to the expense of applying for citizenship in terms of tracking down and acquiring obscure pieces of paper. The time and assistance required to fill in forms (for example, legal help or documentation-checking services) are also considerable investments made by applicants. Jane, who used the documentation-checking facility of the nationality checking service offered by some local authorities, explained:

"I took photocopies of all the supporting documentation and there's a lot: marriage certificates and birth certificates and passports and certificates of registration and blah, blah, blah. So, it's a lot and you always feel a bit nervous just posting those things. So, that was probably the main thing [for going to documentation-checking services], but yes, just, you know, I wanted to be sure that I haven't overlooked anything. Obviously, she's not making a professional judgement about the application [at documentation checking], but she is making sure it is all there. In the final submission [to the Home Office], if you've made a mistake in the application it invalidates it, then you're lost. You've lost all that money.... They [the Home Office] don't ask you to fix it, they reject it and, whether they really do or not, I don't know, but it makes you very nervous, yes."

Catherine, the lawyer in our 'shoemaker and shoes' story in Chapter Three, reported that clients of hers from the European Economic Area (EEA) who are now applying for permanent settlement have to fill in an 89-page form with supporting evidence. Understandably, this has caused distress to many EEA applicants. However, people of other national origins have long been required to fill in lengthy forms. One such person is Sonia, who was born in India to a British mother. She holds British partiality, which entitles her to live in the UK without any restriction (now called the entitlement to the right of abode). Although she has applied for partiality several times, each time lasting for finite periods, she found that the documentation requirements had increased of late:

"… last year, for the first time, I submitted all of my passports from the age of five or four, six, however old I was with my first passport, so I probably submitted about five, six, seven passports, all showing that I had the partiality certificate, which subsequently was called the certificate of entitlement, which subsequently became this entitlement to the right of abode. The difference between previous and this time was I felt the importance of handing in all the passports to prove that I have always had it. I submitted more photographs. I submitted any extra documents I could. Fortunately, I do have all the original birth certificates, death certificates of my parents and all details. I also submitted documents that I own my property in the UK, and I've been paying council tax now since 13 years, in my name. I gave the National Insurance as well. Regardless of how many times I had applied for same certificate successfully in the past each time it is treated as a new one and very first one of its kind. This always makes me extraordinarily nervous. They would take up to six months to make a decision. Can you imagine all these original documents submitted for that long? It is unnerving."

Meticulous documentation – what could even be characterised as 'excessive paperwork' – is mentioned as a defensive strategy by successful applicants. Looking out for gaps and filling them, in anticipation of potential queries, is a very important skill in the citizenship process. It requires personal initiative, as well as the investment of considerable time and money. For Sonia, the documents meant a great deal as she has been safeguarding them ever since her mother developed Alzheimer's disease.

Delay

After the expense of the process and difficulties in evidencing applications through documents of all kinds, the single largest difficulty mentioned by successful applicants is that of delay. Laurie Fransman (2011, p 706) writes in his treatise on British nationality law that at times, because of delays, naturalisation has taken eight years rather than five years in the UK. This rings true from the storytelling data; some applicants report delays of years during which they are kept in the dark about the progress of their applications. In an effort to enquire about their applications, many had involved their MPs, who had phoned or written letters on their behalf to the Home Office and had sometimes been able to gain information. In addition, reconsideration processes for failed applications often dragged on with no decisions, nor any information from the Home Office. The lack of a time frame was also a cause of tremendous anxiety for most applicants. Applicants reported being asked for supporting documents many months after they had submitted their original applications. And often, people were left bewildered when they were asked to resubmit the same documents they had already submitted with their initial application.

Errors

Time delays are often associated with errors in processing applications. At the point of applying for citizenship, people have already been through various stages of visa and leave applications, including the indefinite leave/settlement process. There is considerable room for finding errors in previous visa applications made by the citizenship applicants upon reconsideration. Some applicants, to their 'absolute terror', have been contacted for reasons connected with past successful applications that have been re-scrutinised in light of their citizenship application. For example, an applicant who had already obtained settlement was asked to explain how she had lived only five years in the UK, and she had to point out that she was married to a British citizen so she did not need a sixth year (under the relevant rules at the time). She wondered if she could have simply been rejected without even being given a chance to explain herself. While she felt grateful that she had been allowed to explain the situation, she was upset that the staff at the Home Office dealing with her application did not appear to know the rules themselves. Similarly, in an immigration online forum, 'Ana1986' posted the following comment in August 2016:

I did send my documents with WRS along date 10/5/2008 when applying for PR card. I attached also the letter from my first employer and all p60s for the first years. I don't have any doubts that I acquired PR status in 2013. However, my application was unsuccessful as my card was issued in 15/12/2015. Just hope only my reconsideration will be successful ... Really worried ... It is really confusing that PR card only shows when it was issued not actually the date when a person acquired PR status.

In the end, Ana1986 did not have any problems in acquiring her permanent residence status and it was re-scrutinised after her citizenship application. Similarly, other applicants had been informed that, during certain periods of their life in the UK, they had not had the right to work. When given indefinite leave to remain (ILR) this had been overlooked, but now their citizenship applications were denied as their ILR decisions had wrongly presumed they had the right to work. Several people have successfully contested these determinations in their reconsideration applications by forwarding additional evidence of their right to work. In general, when applicants look back over their strategies, they reflect that evidencing every small detail could make a significant difference to reconsideration applications.

Good character

One of the major reasons for rejections of citizenship applications is the requirement of good character. There are no fixed criteria for this assessment and there is considerable discretion as to how good character is evaluated. However, the stories of successful applicants generally do not dwell on the good character ground as they did not find it difficult to satisfy this requirement. Only one category, those who become citizens after gaining refugee status, were worried about the breadth of this ground. They mentioned how minor traffic issues such as penalty points and fines were causes for concern. They were also concerned that national security material could be introduced in secret to hold back their citizenship. Several high-profile cases involving refugees who were turned down for citizenship served as cautionary tales for other refugees who applied for citizenship:

"There are these cases where the refugees cannot show they have good character just because they were fleeing political regimes and had some contact with resistance groups or had been in trouble with the police in those countries. This is natural, if you are being persecuted. But the British intelligence claimed to have secret evidence on their lack of good character because of these past connections. So, that can happen to anyone. I came here from Egypt when there was so much unrest, I was worried something may be on a file somewhere. Enemies can create problems."

A female respondent in the Scottish report said:

You have to show that you are good person, what you've done for these five years because it's not just so easy just, you apply and they make a decision, as we are asylum seekers you can apply after five years for British citizenship and you have to show what you've done for these five years, so if you, as we were not able to work, okay, we brought all our letters from our colleges, from our volunteering centres, we've just, we've just brought all these papers just and they could see our, each step what we've done. (Quoted in Stewart and Mulvey, 2011, p 54)

In an immigration online forum, in September 2014, 'Serina26' wrote the following:

My application was turned down because of a congestion charge that I appealed. I tried to explain that due to my surgery circumstances, I was not in a position to make a payment for most of the 48 hours allowed to make a payment and that I should be given an extension of 24 hours for my extenuating circumstances. On the same day I received the penalty, I wrote the Congestion Charge explaining my circumstances (see attached evidence on 24th July 2013), but they dismissed it. Since I genuinely felt I had a fair case, I referred the matter to the Traffic Appellate [sic] Authority by completing the necessary forms and posting them. I am self-employed, and this is the only penalty charge I've had during the last 12 years I've been in the UK. They said it affects my 'good character requirements'.

A later post from Serina26 states, 'I managed to get a statement from the adjudicator who issued me with a pcn [parking charge notice] stating that it was not a conviction of any kind so hopefully reconsideration should be successful'. But an even later post highlights her frustration:

Finally got a reply from HO [Home Office]. My reconsideration has been successful after an 8-month battle. I can't believe that the HO employs such an incompetent bunch of people [caseworkers], who don't even know the definition of a conviction/non-custodial sentence. Worse, the HO provides such a bad quality training to its staff. My immigration journey is now over, at last! Thank you to everyone on here. My advice would be: if you feel the wrong decision has been made on your application, don't give up; challenge it and keep fighting. Good luck to all those awaiting a decision.

In relation to good character, applicants have sometimes been asked for documents that go back to their early days in the UK, rather than just the years counted for permanent settlement/indefinite leave. So, for example, some people have had to document their 'good character' for up to a decade, rather than just the previous five or six years, if they have been in the UK for that amount of time. One woman explained:

"I had to fill in a form, I had to submit a lot of proof that I've been living in the UK, a lot of employment details, P45, P60, so I had to contact National Revenue [National Insurance], I had to contact all my colleges that I'd been to, I had to contact my previous employers, any social work department, you know, that were involved with me, it was quite a lot of work, you know, to prove that I've been living here in the last few years and I didn't have any criminal record and stuff like that."

Documenting good character means different things to different people. At one extreme it is interpreted as showing an absence of criminal convictions, at the other as evidencing continuous full employment coupled with volunteering at charities. Although there is no requirement to demonstrate active citizenship (through involvement in civil society activities), applicants sometimes include reference letters to demonstrate their voluntary sector involvement. Even if they are not clear what the expectations are, many applicants mentioned being judged by requirements of conduct much higher than those for other kinds of citizen – for example, those who gain citizenship by birth are not expected to fulfil any criteria of conduct.

Lack of information

With regard to lack of information, Metin, of Turkish origin, narrated the following experience:

"There is no reliable information. The letters and the emails [received during the application process] contained no phone numbers. The Home Office website, that has all sorts of things obviously; I mean the Home Office does include citizenship and naturalisation information. So, there is a phone number you can call. Nationality checking service also provides a phone number, although it's wrong, it's an old number that's not valid."

Shaheeda reported that "... when I called the Home Office about my application, 'No, no, we don't talk to you about that unless it's been here for six months or more'. So, that was the difficult thing". In May 2015, Andrea posted a comment on an online immigration board

about Form NR, which is used for reconsideration of applications in citizenship cases:

> There is not a lot of information out there on how long they typically take and how to get answers from the Home Office. The Home Office have been sitting on my application for about 3 months now and it is getting to the stages where I need my Residence Permit back as proof of my eligibility to work in the UK. No future employer will even entertain my CV without it.

Similarly, refugee applicants who attended a storytelling event expressed annoyance at how difficult it was to understand the intricacies of the operation of the indefinite leave and citizenship pathways. One of them, Altab, said:

> "I'm a refugee from Syria. I've been here for three-and-a-half years, so I feel like I'm one of the early Syrian refugees, and because I spoke English when I arrived here I've been helping all the Syrian community here in the city. Recently people have started to contact me about the indefinite leave but I do not

know … recently I got the job with a city council as a support worker. So, I need to know now and I have no idea how to find out."

Confusion is rampant because of the constant proposals for change. While naturalisation law is codified, there is room in it for use of discretion, Fransman (2011, p 189) points out how naturalisation policy is secret as there is wide discretion to grant or refuse.

Lack of lawyers and legal help

Most applicants who have shared their stories in this book have not accessed any help from legal professionals for their citizenship applications. There are various reasons for this, but the primary reason is expense. However, some applicants find the process relatively straightforward, especially compared with visa applications. For instance, Jane said:

No, I did it myself all the way through. I had a student visa, it was easy. Then I got a work visa, which I was entitled to, and then I applied for leave to remain. Also, I suppose, I was able to navigate it quite easily, because of my education with English as my first language, all of those things. Because the forms are actually quite difficult, and you need to have a lot of resources, I suppose, in terms of time and documentation to substantiate your application. But, yes, so I found it very straightforward."

Many are not aware of whom to approach for assistance. Sonia explained her situation as follows:

"If I'd had a problem, I would have been traumatised, because actually I think that bit isn't so clear. Who do you go to and where are these lawyers who specialise in this, and who is more – who's knowledgeable, understands the law?... Because there's agencies. I've been told there are agents who – in Oxfordshire there's agents here and there's agents there, but who are these agents? It isn't properly listed and it isn't properly documented – their fees and what they actually do and what they actually know isn't even online, I couldn't find any information when I last checked ..."

Many applicants turn to knowledgeable friends or family members to help them navigate the system. Jan, a Polish national resident in Glasgow who applied for British citizenship, said:

"I ended up applying myself. At the time when I was applying my partner was applying as well, and she used to do immigration advice so we were quite confident around the forms. Also, I think what kind of – and in my case, in both our cases it was trouble-free, so – well, aside from the fees, that was the hardest part, I suppose, we managed it."

A couple of applicants had contact numbers of law firms in case of need. Mani, a Sri Lankan by origin, was represented by a leading law firm, hired on his behalf by his employer. However, he researched his own case and eventually found out that his lawyers were giving him incorrect advice. He was deeply disappointed at the quality of legal service from this reputable firm. He said: "My experience has been don't trust any immigration practitioner. There must be some who are good but not sure where they are and whether we can ever know who they are".

Emotional anxiety

Associated with lack of information and the inaccessibility of legal help, is emotional anxiety brought on by the uncertainty of the process. Sonia, while awaiting the renewal of her right of abode, said:

"I became very afraid because my daughter was 16 and still had two years of school and university, and my son was also just finishing university. I felt very vulnerable as they have no other family. I was terrified for the first time about it being rejected, which would be devastating for us as a family. Yes, so that was the process ... there were was no recourse to ring anybody and say – no helpline to say that I was feeling very vulnerable and how long? After the first two weeks passed, you start to get quite nervous and when it came to the end of the first month and then six weeks, I started to get very, very nervous. I really didn't know what was going to happen."

The writer Kamila Shamsie stated in a *Guardian* newspaper article: 'I wasn't prepared for the mutable nature of immigration laws, and their ability to make migrants feel perpetually insecure, particularly as the rhetoric around migration mounted'.[19]

In recent times, the uncertainty of status continues even after gaining citizenship. There are new restrictions in place for family reunion, which means British citizens now have to demonstrate a minimum income in order for their dependants to join them.[20] This has barred thousands from bringing their foreign spouses and children to the UK, as well as elderly, dependent parents (Sumption and Vargas-Silva, 2016).

Even family members who do not seek to enter permanently sometimes have difficulty getting visitor visas. Nadine, who became British after moving to London from South Africa, said:

"My daughter was just looking to come to us for three weeks while she had put in job applications and was waiting for the outcomes. I became a citizen three years back but she is still South African and lives in Jo'burg [Johannesburg]. Would you believe it, they refused her the visa and said you are unlikely to go back? How does that make me feel as a British citizen that my own daughter cannot visit me? I was really sad."

Several British citizens have had to leave in order to follow their families elsewhere as they could not meet the minimum income requirements. Nadine supports herself by working in a spa. She said:

"I will never meet the income requirements for my daughter to join me. But I cannot leave my life here either as there is nothing in South Africa for me to do. Besides, my son works as a trainee chef here. It is such a bind to be in."

The relationships citizens establish with foreigners come up for continuous examination. One story narrated at a storytelling event concerned an attendee's British citizen friend, who has a visual impairment:

"So, he met someone who's Nigerian, and they got married, and you know how the rules are, it's usually easier to go to that person's country to go and get married. So, they got married, and then they applied for her to come over, and then he had to prove that they had a real relationship. The Home Office needed all their emails, every single communication that you have, that you've had, and they picked up one thing he said. Like I said, he's visually challenged, and he's accepting of that fact, so he jokes about it, so he'll say something like, 'I will hit you over the head with my stick'. Of course, he's not going to do that. You know, or he will say, 'Yes, I'm going to tell everyone that you are making fun of a blind man', and he says this to every single person he meets, and then they said, 'Well, it shows that your relationship is not real, and you can't come over'."

The outcome was that the couple did not manage to get together for years and the delay resulted in the end of their marriage.

One participant, Tabitha Sprague,[21] set out the bitter sweetness of her struggle:

"My overall experience has been mixed, but I am struck with an overwhelming feeling of loss. I feel that due to the long wait and my advanced age that I will always be on the bottom step in this country. I will never have the opportunities I should have because I wasn't allowed to settle in the UK at a younger age. Because of this, I don't know if I will ever feel as if I truly belong here. Perhaps time will tell, but I will always wonder, 'What if? What could I have been? What could my life have become without this discrimination?'. My father passed away one year and four days before the law changed. He never lived to see me achieve equality. Thus, I will be moving to the UK with no more support system in place."

Effect of negative experiences on belonging

Mani, of Sri Lankan origin, was employed by an IT company in London on a work permit. At one point, he was outside of the UK for six months on a work assignment, and, as this broke his continuous period of living in the UK, he had to then proffer more evidence to show that he had been in continuous employment during that period and establish that, although he had been in different countries, he had not broken his employment terms. When applying for indefinite leave, Mani gathered all the records of where he had been in the past five years and paid the premium rate for a same-day decision, but his lawyers then advised him not to apply. Not feeling confident about this guidance, he tracked down an unreported legal judgment of a person who had been in exactly his position and who had successfully in obtaining indefinite leave, so, despite the legal advice from the law firm, he went on to submit his application. On his arrival at Lunar House, Croydon, reception staff did not want to let him enter as they had counted how many days he had been in the UK and decided he had not met the required number. Despite their admonishments, he managed to enter and submit his application. He was then kept waiting with his family (including a young child) and, after six hours, was told to go home as there would be no decision that day. Months went by, and eventually Mani contacted his MP, who agreed to intervene. A couple of weeks after his MP had called the Home Office on his behalf, Mani was finally granted indefinite leave to remain. After another year, Mani quite easily obtained citizenship, but he was left deeply scarred by the adversarial nature of the indefinite leave process:

"I felt devalued as a human. It was like my family and I were a nuisance here rather than contributing members of society. It made me feel absolutely not part of British society; like somebody who has to be kept in check. I was paying taxes, national insurance, and working hard to do so, but it did not matter."

Other applicants discussed a sense of regret generated by the application process:

"I regretted the decision to stay here in the first place. At one point, I had options to go elsewhere (Australia and Canada were options) but then I took up the London job, got a mortgage, my child was born. Everything tied me to this country. After I entered the country they extended the requirements for stay in the UK in order to qualify for indefinite leave. I was delayed by two whole years. There is no question of integrating when all you can do is worry about your legal status and you are walking a tightrope all the time."

Participants who referred to expectations of British fairness or a British sense of justice were usually the ones who were most disappointed with the procedures. As Metin said:

"I really expected things to be efficient, very British. Not the way it turned out. I do not believe the immigration system is fit for purpose. My experience was bad but when looking up my situation I read about many who suffered much more. It made me scared of being here."

Sonia, who holds a partiality certificate (now rarely issued), said:

> "Once, at Heathrow airport, I was approached a few years ago by a gentleman who asked to see my passport, out of the blue. He saw my certificate and asked me how I had been entitled to that, if I could explain. I found it quite scary, quite frightening. It was an official, a plain-clothed official, who just stepped out. They were just observing people coming into the airport. I had to explain about my grandparents and my mother and my children being British. He said, 'Fine, it seems to be on many counts that you've got this entitlement', so that was fine, but it is not correct. My entitlement is very specific to partiality in line of descent, which is through my grandparents being born in the UK. But for a few minutes I felt like I had no right to being here."

A similar loss of sense of belonging is also reported by BB from Cameroon, who stated in the *Guardian* online ('Immigrants in their own words – 100 stories',[22] 'I do not call myself British because of what I went through getting this passport. Those experiences are part of who I am and I only share them with other immigrants who can relate'.

Bureaucracy and citizenship

The various reasons for loss of confidence in the nationality process are closely connected to its bureaucratic nature. Ewick and Silbey (1998, p 185) write that: 'Bureaucracies make actions indecipherable because of no standard operating procedures, no taxonomies classifying or forbidding such practices'. The murkiness of sources of information and of timescales for outcomes appear to be part of this bureaucratic scheme.

Georgina, whose children's biometric information was swapped around in error, explained:

"It felt very much like a bureaucracy for me in the worst possible way. So, it didn't feel like there were legal principles at stake here, it felt like they were administrative, bureaucratic problems and that's how I experienced it."

Her problem was resolved in the end. She continued:

"Then one day I get an email from, I can't remember her name but she was an actual person at last, an actual person at the Home Office. I don't know why she picked it up but she said, 'Could you please re-send me the PDFs of the applications and I'll look into this', and within about two to three days it was sorted. But it was a person, it was the same person who went back and forth and allowing me to communicate with the same person as opposed to the biometric email address, without a – she gave me a personal email address, it was a Home Office address but it wasn't the biometric one."

This personal intervention made the difference to her applications, but came after many months of failed efforts and battling automatic replies from generic email addresses.

Thom from the US wrote online:[23]

Navigating my way through visa applications was a mess. Few seemed to have any clear understanding of the rules. While everyone in the media seems to think there are few regulations, the truth is there is a tsunami of rules that seemed designed to keep people out by tricking them on some technicality ...

At a storytelling event, Bill analysed his experience of applying for indefinite leave as follows:

"No. It didn't feel overly legal. It felt more bureaucratic than legal, if you accept or if I can draw a distinction between those things. Yes, I didn't think about it in those terms. It felt like a bureaucracy and it felt like a bureaucracy particularly in the post submission stage."

Here, Bill's description of the process as bureaucracy is a pejorative one, nearly synonymous with delay, complicated rules and lack of responsiveness, rather than being a merely descriptive one of institutional structure.

Sameness, national identity and naturalisation procedures

Underlying the challenges of expense, delay and bureaucratic is a more conceptual problem of presumed sameness of what it means to become British for every applicant irrespective of their background. Long-term migrants get trapped between understandings of sameness and difference. Andreouli and Dashtipour (2014) explain this as the use of naturalisation legislation in a nation-building project in Britain; citizenship, more than a set of formal rights and duties, is thereby linked to the creation of a uniform national identity. While integration may be the goal, Tyler writes that naturalisation procedures are also used to 'govern' migrant populations so that less desirable ones can never join the citizenry (Tyler, 2010). The oath-taking ceremony, for instance, can be seen as an example of the suspicion governments have of migrants who may have alternate loyalties.

Democratically elected majoritarian states and their agencies can express the national popular will, which is often expressly anti-immigrant and anti-diversity (Miller, 1997). As a result, applicants like Roberta, when put to the test in this manner, feel stripped of their Britishness rather than reinforced in their sense of belonging. She said:

"Yes, legally I was from Botswana and only now have put in my citizenship application but in uni no one treated me as not British. The application process has now made me feel foreign. I am bit un-British, if you know what I mean. It took away my sense of feeling [British] because of the steps I had to take, all the money my family spent."

Similarly, the Scottish report (Stewart and Mulvey, 2011) demonstrates how candidates for citizenship view the requirements. One respondent (EM2) said: 'It's rubbish, to be candid … it's just a ceremony, to be candid, just ceremonious things that we done there and that's it.… It didn't mean anything' (quoted in Stewart and Mulvey, 2011, p 48). Refugees who are driven out of their homelands are likely to opt for citizenship out of a sense of compulsion. The report points out how some of the interviewees did not even realise there was an option not to take up citizenship. The sense of compulsion and obligation negates any real sense of loyalty or belonging that the procedures might have hoped to have engendered in applicants.

What explains the disaffectation of applicants? Partly, it is the bureaucratic approach of officials, but also, as we saw in Chapters 1 and 2, expectations of 'sameness' affect minority citizens. To demonstrate the effects of these expectations on the citizenship application processes, here is the narrative of Roberta from Botswana, a graduate of Leeds University:

> "Yes, I had to do the language tests, even though I went to Leeds University, which is a rather good university, and because I'm from Botswana I can't speak English, apparently [said sarcastically], and I don't know what English is. It's just small things like that which is very frustrating; very frustrating. For a lot of people, it's a mountain of small things, and then the rules change and you have to do another mountain of small things at your own expense."

Roberta feels British. She fully identifies as British. She even attended boarding school in the Midlands for several years. The application process for her was important only for acquiring a passport as her Botswana passport did not allow her to travel visa-free in Europe. As a university graduate, she resented the language requirement tests and was annoyed that she could not get an exemption from them. What caused her discomfort was that she had to demonstrate her Britishness through these crude tests, while she clearly felt the same as any other young British person. Ironically, she had to undertake a conversation examination in which she conversed on the topic of university life. She was bitter about that experience and mocked it by making dark jokes: "So my conversation test made me think, how did I manage to converse for three years in uni, duh?". She also observed the distressed older applicants who were in her examination centre. They were rooted in specific migrant communities and lacked fluency in English. They were desperately learning pre-prepared conversation scripts as they could not improvise in English conversations. It troubled her that they were being traumatised by this requirement at an advanced age and often while suffering from physical ailments. Roberta reflected:

> "I understand language is important but clearly the older people were being cared for by family and their communities and were getting by that way. This was just hardship for them. Like me, they should have had some sort of exemption as well."

Roberta is another example of someone who feels British and identifies as British without possessing citizenship in law. Her experience highlights the presumption of sameness in naturalisation procedures. Roberta was annoyed at the lack of exemptions from tests, but at least she could establish her own language credentials quite easily. Many family dependants, such as the elderly applicants Roberta encountered, find it difficult to meet these requirements. Yet, family members are insiders in society through established networks of relations and already have moral claims (Carens, 2003, p 97).

Schweitzer (2015) writes that family reunification can never just be a matter of immigration control, but constitutes a human rights issue as well. When spouses or elderly parents have to demonstrate 'integration' through language proficiency, it creates 'racialised' patterns of civic stratification. There are also gender dimensions to family migration, and integration measures generally disadvantage women. Wray (2015) writes that the bias in family migration is that men are generally regarded as economic agents and family is viewed as marginal to their lives, and this means that it is hard for them to establish or re-establish family relations in the UK.

The efficacy of integration requirements such as the citizenship test and language tests has also been questioned by scholars and applicants alike. Tests purport to prepare applicants for civic life through providing practical knowledge of the country and fellow citizens as well as better language skills for active engagement. Gray and Griffin (2014) write that the Home Office view is that citizenship is more valued if it is earned and not just given. Tests contribute to both earning and learning citizenship. However, earning and learning are contradictory functions because integration is furthered by becoming a citizen rather than merely being a by-product of preparations for citizenship tests. Holding people back via the test requirements hampers their future integration.

In the Scottish report, two female respondents (GF5/6) stated: 'Pass test, they forgot everything ... I think yes, it's waste time' (quoted in Stewart and Mulvey, 2011, p 51). For them, knowledge of life in the UK can only come from living in the UK, rather than from reading books and then taking tests. Brooks (2016, pp 106-7) writes that the exam booklets themselves often contain wrong information or leave out practical instructions.

Bill, the economics professor of American origin based in London, provides an account of the citizenship test:

"So, the Labour test was about how you open a bank account, what are your rights as a tenant, what are your rights as a landlord, things like that, and there was a little, very short history at the beginning of it but it wasn't part of the test, in the book that you revised. It was a disappointing history in many respects, predictable respects, but – you know, discussion of industrialisation without mention of poverty or something like that. So, everyone thinks you have to be ashamed of parts of your history that are not necessarily glorious, right, so there is nothing about colonialism or racism, nothing about race relations, nothing about riots, nothing about anything like this. I think that's really unfortunate for those things that are left out of it, not because those are the most important parts of the history, but because it looks like you're trying to present this rosy picture of something that just isn't. I think it ends up looking like propaganda, which it is and a more balanced historical account would be much – a country confident enough to come to terms with it. Which it clearly has in many ways, so there is public discourse about imperialism, colonialism, racism, these sorts of things, but I think there needs to be some of it there as well. Or, there was mention of suffrage, universal suffrage for women, and not talking about – so they make it sound like, well, from 1929 or whatever the date was, I've probably forgotten, but that women are equal. Well, of course they're not and so glossing over history in this way; no discussion of gender parity, no discussion of anything. I understand the main purpose is to instil a sense of pride in people but a sense of pride that's based on a distorted understanding of history is not a very useful sense of pride."

Bill's criticism of the focus on trivia, rather than more significant details, and the skimping on difficult periods of history are two recurrent ideas about citizenship tests that appear in the stories of applicants who took them.

Citizenship ceremony: negative experiences

The final step towards citizenship is a citizenship ceremony. The ceremony consists of an oath or affirmation of allegiance to the Crown and a pledge of loyalty to the UK: '... a formal promise to Her Majesty the Queen and the United Kingdom'. For many applicants, this experience is a pleasurable one. The stories in the next chapter illustrate that the citizenship ceremony is the highlight of the citizenship journey for most applicants. Some, however, resent having to take oaths that citizens by birth do not have to take. As one participant said: "The purpose is to just test our fidelity. Why, after we have already lived so long here? Why the need to make promises?".

Writer Kamila Shamsie explained the political duplicity as follows:

We had all been given envelopes for our certificates, and when I opened mine out popped Theresa May. Or at least a letter of welcome from her, with her photograph at the top of the page. Just a few weeks earlier, May had sent her 'Go Home' vans[24] across the UK, so this hardly inspired a feeling of belonging. Instead, it served as a reminder that the process of coming to British citizenship through six years of residence can't really be a process of feeling increasingly British when it is so marked with threat and insecurity.[25]

Bridget Byrne writes in her book *Making citizens* (2014, p 114) that, although the Home Office has no role in organising citizenship ceremonies, many applicants she interviewed at the ceremonies thought that the ceremonies were organised by the Home Office. Although local registrars do much to make the event welcoming, some future citizens still consider the process to be continued immigration control. Byrne (2014) found this to be true even of elite and transnational migrants who have support for their applications from their employers and families. Some of them were reluctant to be interviewed by her while waiting for their citizenship ceremonies. There was considerable fear of any kind of assessment even at this ultimate stage of citizenship.

In any case, future citizens do not all afterwards experience the same kind of welcome that they are accorded in the ceremonies, as illustrated by Jane, one of the storytelling event participants:

> "After the ceremony, in a private conversation, the Lord Mayor told me, 'Well, it's an honour to welcome you, which is more than I can say for some of the other people here'. I am a white, Canadian-origin woman. And, she was looking at some non-Caucasian people when she spoke to me. So, I was a bit afraid for what it meant, and it ruined it for me. It was ugly, and it was actually gross misconduct, if you ask me."

While such tales of blatant racism are rare, the ceremony experience is highly variant from place to place, with participants reporting there was very little in the welcome ceremonies to do with national values or belonging in any deep sense.

Conclusion

People who shared warm stories about belonging in the previous chapter have often also shared tales of bureaucracy and inefficiency in this chapter. The multiple stories people share include similar hurdles such as the expense of naturalisation and legal advice, detailed bureaucratic approaches to applications, lack of information, lack of legal advice, and problems with time requirements. These experiences harm people's sense of belonging and defeat any goals of 'integration' or of furthering understanding of 'British values' or of celebrating 'multiculturalism'. On the positive side, the stories highlight people's resilience, determination and coping strategies. It appears that naturalisation processes favour those who are able to demonstrate these qualities, rather than displaying fairness and non-discrimination. In the chapter that follows, however, we will find reinforcement of belonging for a select few.

FIVE

A few fairy tales? Stories of success

Drawing from the stories of applicants, the previous chapter provided some insight into the negative experiences associated with citizenship applications. A number of challenges clearly exist on the road to naturalisation. Given that these are the stories of successful applicants, it seems logical that the experiences of failed applicants must be far worse. Narrations of how citizenship applications proceed are, however, not uniformly bleak. There are a few applicants who report finding the process an empowering one. Some applicants enjoy certain aspects of the citizenship journey, even if, overall, they experience anxiety and stress. While the data on positive experiences is far outweighed by the evidence on negative experiences of applicants, it is worth examining what makes the process positive for at least some individuals sometimes. Perhaps then it will be possible to replicate these successfully for others as well.

Vanessa's story

"I am the sort of person who likes challenges so this was good for me. This challenge of ticking each citizenship box. I enjoyed the Life in the UK test.... It was good to read up for. I was so impressed with the quality of my fellow test takers ... best brains from round the world (scientists, doctors, teachers). The funny bit happened when I found a spelling mistake in the test and emailed Home Office to tell them. They emailed me back thanking me!"

The most positive account of the citizenship application process in this study comes from Vanessa, a professional of Kenyan origin. Vanessa had been moving countries since she was a one-year-old baby. Her parents moved to Madrid from Nairobi on diplomatic passports. They lived there for around five years and then moved back to Kenya. Vanessa lived in Kenya until 2007 and then moved to Nigeria with her husband. A few years later the couple decided to come to the UK as Vanessa's husband was planning to take up an academic post there. Vanessa arrived first on a Tier 1 visa, valid for two years, and quickly found a job in the healthcare sector. Her husband kept postponing his trip and eventually refused to join her, instead seeking separation. Now they are divorced.

Vanessa's life plans had taken an unexpected turn. She could have returned to Kenya and resumed her old life there, but, instead, she looked for a better-paid job in London, took help from her parents to buy a small flat, and decided to make her own life in that city. The global recession hurt her employment prospects, but she was determined to secure suitable work. At one point, she juggled three part-time jobs to make ends meet.

Five years after securing a permanent job, Vanessa successfully obtained indefinite leave to remain (ILR). A year later, she applied for citizenship, and, in her own words, 'breezed through it'. She was very proud to make it alone in a city she feels is her own. What allowed Vanessa to experience the citizenship journey on such positive terms? She too had numerous forms to fill in and expenses to meet during the application process. She had the exact same requirements to fulfil as other applicants, but her attitude was always positive and resilient. However, despite her upbeat story and personality, Vanessa is internally a worrier. In terms of preparation, she paid great attention to detail and overprepared each aspect of the application. She worried about all eventualities and tried to counter the negative ones. She explained her strategy for her citizenship application as follows:

"I flooded Home Office with paperwork. I documented each bit of my life so they could not reject me. If they wanted bank statements of three years, good, I gave them five years' worth. Can't harm, can it? I got all kinds of letters: from work, from travels. Each day of absence, I accounted for carefully. It would have been difficult to find anything missing."

Vanessa continued:

"The Home Office are just bureaucrats. They need to tick boxes so they need backup evidence. It is best to give them what they need in an organised manner. Have no gaps. Make your story easy to understand."

Vanessa comprehends the bureaucratic process well because her parents had jobs in the diplomatic service and were situated within bureaucracies. She says bureaucratic offices can provide service, but they have to be "used properly".

There is always a backstory to stories of migration. Given the preparation that went into her application process, it was interesting to investigate how Vanessa had arrived in London and what preparations she had made for her visa. Vanessa had travelled numerous times to London in her life and she already knew that she would be happy to live there.

"It is a global city. I could choose Berlin or another large German city as I know German. Or I could choose London. I did think carefully about Germany, but German citizenship is much harder to achieve. I was making a move for settling down. I had travelled too much in my life and did not want to just move for the sake of moving. Kenya, Nigeria and all other places were great, but I was restless for the global city life."

She had her life well documented before she applied for her visa. She said: "This is my instinctive nature. I had an auditor audit all my money". When her parents helped her purchase her London flat, she ensured the money was fully documented and accounted for by her accountant. She did not want it to cause any concerns in her citizenship process; any unexplained cash flows could be potentially interpreted as money laundering. While she was on her visa, every time she travelled she had her employer's human resources department certify that each trip was for work.

Vanessa also used the internet and joined online discussion forums when she had any queries. ILR requirements were subject to change and government websites were often contradictory. As a result, on one occasion she had contacted the Home Office via email and after two weeks received a reply that was not particularly helpful as it merely referred her back to the confusing guidance section that had prompted her query in the first place. She decided to use documentation-checking services, mainly for access to the accelerated service that runs alongside document checking. However, she did not find the service useful as her documents were not properly examined. She had also provided much more information than the document-checking service had requested – explanations for everything and even extra documents. Subsequently, it took her two months to get her passport back. She said that the Home Office website was chaotic, but people in the Croydon office were very friendly when she went there to submit her applications.

The most important element in Vanessa's story is her positive attitude to the demanding requirements of citizenship applications. Whereas most people would say, 'I hate filling in forms', she said, "For me, it was an adventure. And what could happen in the worst case?". What is behind her positive spirit? To a large extent it is her own personality and associated life experiences, but a pertinent structural point is also that she had a sense of security about her life back in Kenya. She was not scared of returning to Kenya. She was solely motivated by a spirit of adventure. Having the choice was a privilege for her:

"I just wanted to prove I could do this professionally. Be properly grown up and capable. Make my own life. But I was not running away from anything so that was not so hard for me."

Vanessa's story opens up a number of discussion points, the first being the expectations people have of their new lives and how these experiences may bolster feelings of belonging. This matches up with other accounts on belonging already explored in Chapter Three. Clearly, Vanessa is one of those who seeks to reinvent themselves or consolidate their own lives, while at the same time seeking to imbibe different cultures and values. Therefore, her own cosmopolitan outlook helps create her 'Britishness' and sense of belonging in London.

Apart from her positive approach, Vanessa also understands the nature of bureaucracies and how to use this to her advantage. This leads us to the second major discussion point arising out of the story: the nature of bureaucracies.

Bureaucracy as game

Vanessa's ability to negotiate the application process at each step of the immigration and nationality procedure is connected to her view of bureaucracies as places where one has to strategically negotiate end results. At every point, she assessed relevant rules to understand how these would be operationalised by Home Office agents. She imagined their actions on receipt of her papers: What checklists would they have to fill? What kind of files would they open? What evidence would they need to assess her forms according to the relevant guidance? Vanessa sought to pre-empt problems and anticipate difficulties.

Vanessa's actions are very similar to those of a character in Patricia Ewick and Susan Silbey's book, *The common place of law: Stories from everyday life* (1998). Like Vanessa, this character, Nikos Stravos, was battling the bureaucratic approach of the law by thinking of counter-strategies:

Nikos left little to chance. The tactics that he had learned earlier – the importance of documents and reliance on the resources made available by other organisations – were skilfully employed in constructing his case. (Ewick and Silbey, 1998, p 125)

Meticulous documentation was part of his plan for 'using the law'.

Vanessa, like Nikos, fundamentally believes that bureaucrats deliver results that, in the end, could serve a useful purpose, but that they do so only after labyrinthine procedures are set in motion. In the words of Ewick and Silbey (1998, p 91), bureaucratic services also have capacity: the productive side of legality. However, bureaucrats are aware of the limits of their capacity and use the procedures to sort out who will be the 'haves' and who will be the 'have-nots'. This reality – of winners and losers and complicated rules that can be played with – renders bureaucratic processes into games.

An online immigration board post from Varunadas (in March 2015) also demonstrates how strategic thinking can be key to positive outcomes:

My wife had absences of 735 days and we applied for exemption based on my son not [being] well and had to be out of country for medical treatment as there was a long delay at NHS [National Health Service]. They asked for detailed medical records from overseas doctors and approved the application. I believe that if you have sufficient grounds with valid evidence they generally consider as it is not always possible for every applicant to satisfy the 450-day qualifying criteria for absence. We did delay her application by a year after her arrival to ensure we fulfil the absences criteria in the last 12 months and used that as a basis to explain our intent to get based over here.

Here, there was a rule, but there was also scope for the use of discretion, and Varunadas was able to provide evidence that brought his wife's application within the range of that discretion. The application was also timed strategically, so that it was possible to demonstrate intent to reside in the UK.

Money, resources, privilege

Applicants who had positive experiences while applying for citizenship were not just resourceful in their use of strategies, but also had resources to smoothen the process. Applicants can choose to pay for expedited services. Appeals and reviews, wherever available, all incur fees, and legal assistance is expensive. Vanessa, for instance, spent £1,800 for an accelerated ILR. Money made the process much easier for her. She contrasted her situation with that of a close friend from South Africa, who is struggling because her husband is unemployed. She has to reapply for her visa every two years and is trying to remain in the UK for 10 years in order to regularise her status.

Class and race also intersect in interesting ways. Two applicants (both of white European descent) said in a storytelling event that they were contacted directly by the Home Office when they failed to fill in some details of their form. For example, one applicant said:

> "The only time the Home Office phoned me was because they said there was a discrepancy on the forms, and then I thought, 'Oh gosh, I've put up all this money and it's going to get rejected', but it was actually because they were confused because on my passport it had the neighbourhood where I was born, but I had filled in the city where I was born."

The other reported that "I was contacted because my middle name varied slightly in the form from my passport".

An immigration lawyer in the audience responded as follows:

> "That's interesting as none of my poorer clients would ever be called to correct their forms! I think these are the points where privilege really comes to play, your class, your race, your

background. I think it more gets overlooked if you're ... class and/or white, and from Europe, as opposed to ... for example, from Afghanistan."

The application process: what works well

Some applicants manage to undergo the process only because of their firm faith in the British system. Graham, of Australian origin, felt he could submit all his original documents without much fear and said:

"Yes, because my faith was in the system that, if it's been issued, there will be a record surely that it's been issued all these years back, and my documents and my grandparents' and parents' records would be there. I trust that these wouldn't have altered in anyway. I was trusting that there was a record of all that and therefore I wouldn't need to take any legal recourse. And, it did work out that way."

Similarly, applicants praised services like the nationality checking service, offered by some local authorities to check applications for British citizenship, which was described as 'good and very thorough'. Another applicant described the service as follows:

"The interaction at nationality checking service was not the robotic, bureaucratic kind but one that was good in terms of their professionalism and, not only their professionalism but because there's a lot of time given to applicants. We were chatting at different points when photocopies were being made or whatever, different things. So, I said some of my views about the process and in a very sincere way there was a sympathetic response like, yes, she sees these people come in shaking like a leaf and she tells them they don't have to be scared but at the same time she understands the situation that I described, existential angst about, what happens if it's unsuccessful, or, you know. Sometimes you can get someone on the phone at the Home

Office, they're professional, they're kind, they're helpful. It hasn't been so many times that I've rung them but when I have, I've always had positive experiences, if I can get them on the phone. So, the nationality checking service was fine, it was thorough."

Another participant commented positively on how Home Office staff dealt with queries, and was delighted to find that telephone calls were "not outsourced" (directed to remote call centres):

"Staff were knowledgeable, confident, polite, friendly. I probably made two or three calls and each time the experience was positive. It was a good way to get a quick question resolved and you didn't need a lawyer, you could get more useful information from the Home Office itself on these things."

Positive views on the requirements of tests

The benefits of citizenship beyond ILR come across strongly in this set of stories. Vanessa enjoyed the Life in the UK test, which she said was "good to read up for". She was impressed with the quality of fellow test takers, saying that they were the best brains from around the world (scientists, doctors and teachers).

Other applicants also found the information in the Life in the UK test interesting, with one participant commenting: "Even if it is a potted history one does learn some highlights of history". Some applicants (who themselves did not have to take the language test) were emphatic that English language skills need to be tested: "Surely speaking English is crucial if you want to get around here?". In a Scottish report on refugees who became citizens (Stewart and Mulvey, 2011), one applicant for citizenship (GM17) said: '… it's embarrassing as well to say that you are British, but you can't even speak English language which is, basically, English is the British language … everybody has to learn the language, has to be able to communicate properly' (quoted in Stewart and Mulvey, 2011, p 49).

Positive experiences of the citizenship ceremony

For most applicants, the citizenship ceremony is a significant one as it is the ultimate step towards citizenship. Bridget Byrne (2014) writes that the citizenship ceremony marked the end of a long bureaucratic process for her interviewees. Her research participants tended to downplay negative effects of the citizenship process once they had succeeded (2014, p 113). Storytelling participant Bill, the academic of American origin, expressed his feelings as follows:

> "I like coming to big football matches and getting that kind of experience of the crowd. So, the collective thing is quite nice. It was the recent mayoral elections as well so it was this sort of spontaneous celebration of multiculturalism ... there were 45 people from 25 different countries and you really appreciate that. This is nice to see these people becoming citizens because they're not part of the problem, they're part of the solution, and so there is kind of this – yes, it's nice. So, I did appreciate the ceremony.

Vanessa, whose story was narrated at the beginning of the chapter, enjoyed the solemnity of swearing an oath: "It was a little bit like getting married, although more like a group event. I enjoyed the pomp of ceremonial officialdom. Was so emotional by the end".

Stories of the ceremony describe the tea, biscuits and ceremonial officers as particularly British aspects. But Oreos, instant coffee, and the presence of huge flags were deemed un-British and were not generally appreciated. Migrant–citizens liked speeches that underlined multiculturalism. Alina recollected a speech as follows:

> "'We don't tolerate racism, we don't tolerate discrimination', and I was glad to hear that. There were some other things about, you know, 'Don't break the rules and don't commit any crimes and don't be terrorists', and things like that said in a subtler manner than how I am putting now. Fair enough, although someone

who has worked hard and naturalised is hardly likely to be first in queue to do random acts of violence, don't you think?"

Catherine spoke fondly of her experience of the citizenship ceremony:

"So I was particularly touched that the Lord Mayor who did a wonderful job – perhaps more aspirational, welcoming all sorts of different people and encouraging living together harmoniously. There was a portrait of the Queen, and we could all have our photograph taken, with the Lord Mayor, and the picture of the Queen. The best bit was that the Home Office guy, when it was time to have the National Anthem, he went over to press a button on a creaky old boom-box, and a sudden burst started, and he had to run over quickly and [laughs] – so that was the cheesiest. But it was genuinely moving as well, especially being alongside the other people who were there, with all those different stories coming into that one place."

Many applicants remembered the details of the room and their fellow citizens that day, describing the event in a vivid manner:

"The decor, but also there was a table draped with the Union Jack flag, and then there were two Union Jacks sticking out of it. It was basically a Union Jack on a Union Jack, and I was like, right [laughs]. Then the room was just full of people. I think there were 30 people in 18 nationalities in the room, which I thought was great, and actually – because I'm being quite flippant, but to me that was the best –– it is about Britain, really. So that bit was very important ... and I'm very happy to be here with all those people becoming British for all sorts of different reasons. Then there was also a Jamaican lady sat next to me, and she was wearing a beautiful dress, and we're just so different, because I generally dress casually, and I was casually dressed, and it was really interesting to see how different people were at the ceremony. Some people were very casual, like they just came from a shift at work, and others were really dressed up for the occasion. There was also a Queen representative there as well, some lady with a very posh accent."

All these differences were embraced by migrant–citizens who felt that they served to underline the multicultural identity of modern-day Britain.

Confirmation of belonging

While most migrant–citizens desire citizenship for the obvious benefits – passport, enhanced ability to work and right to vote – the citizenship process engenders greater belonging for some applicants. Adaoma, who, as we discovered in Chapter Two, had carried her blue suitcase full of papers to many law offices, said:

"I went through so many challenges getting my visa renewals. Was out of job at one point and thought would have to leave. It was hard. Getting ILR was so difficult. I was mentally exhausted from it. But citizenship was like a dream and made me so proud. I could forget all the past problems. I was free."

Vanessa, too, felt empowered by her citizenship process. She gained confidence in herself when she finished the citizenship ceremony and picked up her passport. Tabitha Sprague, the participant who talked about her experiences with mixed feelings in Chapter Four, reminisced:

"What makes me happy is that I finally have my passport. It represents my much-deserved birthright. It proves that I truly am British. My passport also represents more opportunities for my life as I'm now a dual UK/US citizen. I received my Certificate of British Citizenship on August 11, 2016, at the Consulate in New York. It was an emotional experience (to say the least!) and I broke down during the part of the oath where I had to say the word 'British citizen'. Some nights later, when [tennis player] Andy Murray won the Olympic Gold, I thought to myself how nice it was he won. Then, I got an overwhelming feeling of excitement when I realised that I am now officially British and I cheered him on – as a Brit!"

Conclusion

In Chapter Three the data indicated that the most effective determiner of belonging is length of residence. Once people have lived in the UK for long while, they imbibe a sense of belonging. Any tests that attempt to create belonging are too late in the citizenship journeys. So what does determine whether a person feels stripped of a sense of Britishness, or whether they happen to acquire an extra layer of Britishness, through the citizenship procedures? It is hard to tell as the data varies. Chapter Four demonstrated that, clearly, difficulties in applying for citizenship may reduce a sense of belonging. But, causality cannot be readily determined as there are exceptions to this trend as well. From the stories, it appears there is a correlation between how people felt before they applied and their subsequent experience of the procedures. In nearly all the stories when people already felt they were British or had a claim to British identity (even if through past heritage, such as colonial connections), they saw the application process as a general challenge rather than one designed to exclude them in a targeted manner. When they lacked a sense of belonging or connection to Britain, however, they were much more likely to feel personally excluded by the legal procedures. In some instances, people had an acquired sense of belonging that was damaged by their application experience and their perception of 'unfairness' of treatment.

The following chapter concludes the book by summarising general trends and proposing some policy recommendations so that future cohorts of migrant–citizens are not hemmed in by bureaucracy but become a welcome part of British citizenry.

SIX

And they lived happily ever after? Some conclusions ...

The legal and sociological basis of membership

Britishness, belonging and citizenship: Experiencing nationality law has explored the links between sociological understandings of belonging and formal, legal citizenship. The relationship between the two is complex and multidimensional. By contrast, citizenship and belonging are often reduced to stereotypical, binary ideas of inclusion and exclusion. The image of the immigrant–stranger who is an outsider and the citizen–member who is an insider is inadequate for capturing the complexity of citizenship (Schuck, 1998, p 475). Instead, a variety of positions on being, and becoming citizens, and on experiencing belonging, can be traced as part of a membership continuum in modern-day Britain.

Another binary depiction is that of the country as the giver of all benefits and of the migrant as the receiver of all benefits of membership (Dummett and Nicol, 1990, p 4). What migrants bring in terms of skills, experience and knowledge remains greatly undervalued.

Another noteworthy point is that belonging is not exclusively experienced as national citizenship; it could merely be about feeling at home in a neighbourhood, experiencing a connection to a city, or closeness to other people.

Findings on belonging

While citizenship can be depicted as a gateway to full membership in society, data in this book demonstrates that there are various kinds and degrees of belonging that do not always run parallel with secure legal status. The emotions of belonging are not always associated with securing citizenship in law. Rogers Brubaker (1992, p 36) writes:

Formal citizenship is neither a sufficient nor a necessary condition for substantive membership.... That it is not a sufficient condition is clear: one can possess formal state membership yet be excluded (in law or in fact) from certain civil, political, or social rights.

In addition, the stories in this book manifest that, in the absence of full formal citizenship, it is still possible to have intense feelings of belonging. Just as nations are built on imagined communities, migrants imagine nations and neighbourhoods based on their own expectations and experiences prior to their migration journey. On arrival, when there is a fit between their expectations and experiences, they are likely to develop closer associations and deepen their sense of belonging.

Britishness

For many successful applicants, citizenship is the culmination of a lifetime of effort; the process merely formally recognises their pre-existing strong relationship with Britain and their already socialised sense of Britishness. There are clear indications that Britishness is understood by most applicants as an inclusive value; not one measured in just years lived here, but also in terms of inherited qualities and values. Sometimes, these are inherited from older members of family who experienced various forms of British subjecthood in earlier times. For those who arrive from former British colonies, these are common experiences as they have a heritage drawn from childhood memories, history, or representations in books and media.

Value of formal, legal citizenship

Whatever their background, gaining citizenship is a vital target for many long-term migrants. As Thom Brooks observes (2016, p 276), British citizenship matters to British people. Once non-citizens legally enter the UK, depending on their visa status, they are subject to specific conditions. These conditions apply until they gain settled status (European Economic Area [EEA] nationals) or indefinite leave to remain (ILR) (non-EEA nationals). Until citizenship is secured, however, the leave to remain or settled status can be revoked if residents leave the country for more than two years or become subject to criminal law proceedings. Only citizenship provides freedom from all immigration controls. As citizenship is the most secure status in law, gaining it is a moment of great consequence for applicants.

Gaps in citizenship pathways

The stories in this book are of successful citizenship applicants, but not everyone can readily access the security offered by citizenship. Unskilled migrants have little opportunity in the immigration system for gaining secure status (Andreouli and Dashtipour, 2014). Bridget Anderson (2010) writes that, for precarious workers, immigration controls create categories of entrance and institutionalise uncertainty.

Yet, this book demonstrates that routes available to long-term resident migrants are far from being fair and transparent and are also fraught with uncertainty. Although migrant–citizens are longer-term residents of a more resilient kind, they undergo similar experiences of bureaucratic categorisation and institutionalised uncertainty in their journeys to citizenship. For many, the citizenship journey is a protracted form of immigration control that continues right up until the point of the citizenship ceremony. With the rise in cancellation of citizenship for naturalised citizens for national security reasons, there is the possibility of life-long monitoring of the conduct of migrant–citizens. Therefore, in the British context, the procedures of citizenship are about the politics of belonging (inclusion and exclusion), rather than real belonging in the sense of territorial, relational and emotive membership (Yuval-Davis, 2011).

Migrants who successfully become migrant–citizens negotiate uncertainty through a combination of resources and resourcefulness. But why should they have to overcome such barriers? Why should there not be systemic safeguards in place instead to ensure simplicity and efficacy of legal procedures and widespread availability of support in making applications?

Role of civil society

In the absence of such systemic safeguards, the missing narrative in most people's citizenship stories is that of the presence of supportive and collaborative civil society organisations and groups. There are very few organisations in the UK that can provide support to long-term residents. Brooks (2016, p 276) writes: 'Becoming British has become a solitary exercise conducted between the individual and the state. It misses out the general public in the middle. This must be corrected'. Unlike the US, where there are social and political movements for inclusion in American legal residence and citizenry (such as United We Dream, which is a large youth-led movement), there are very few social movements or organisations for citizenship rights in the UK. One exception is the Project for the Registration of Children as British Citizens (PRCBC), which has spearheaded the inclusion of long-term resident children as British citizens. Such organisations sustain the efforts made by individuals who are at risk of falling through the cracks of nationality provisions. One person who has benefited from the help of PRCBC and, in turn, generated a network for support of excluded children, is research participant Tabitha Sprague, who says:

> "If it weren't for the hard work of PRCBC, through Lord Avebury's amendment (which changed the 'scope of the law' in the House of Lords), I honestly don't know if this law would have changed when it did ... I am a UKF applicant [person born before 1 July 2006 to a British father and whose parents were not married] who is proud to have had a hand in overturning the discriminatory requirement in the BNA [British Nationality Act] 1981 that both parents had to be married in order to acquire UK citizenship through a British born father and a non-British mother. In 2009, frustrated with the government's latest unsuccessful attempt to change the law, I set up a personal blog with the original intent to 'name and shame' ... I was even more surprised that nobody publicly advocated for us or challenged the government on their words and actions. This

discrimination should never have been able to have gone on as long as it did. There were several opportunities to change such an unfair law, and each time the subject was broached during a Bill in Parliament the amendment would be quashed. I started my blog because I couldn't find much in the way of support from immigration and human rights advocates. Through my blog I met several others in my position and although we were a small group, we became close. More importantly, I have met so many people through campaigning. Our group may be small, but we have a huge amount of love between us. That is also what inspires me and makes me so happy to have fought for equality. Those bonds between us and our shared experiences will never weaken."

From Tabitha's story, it is evident that solidarity and organisational support are key to achieving fair and equal access to citizenship. Although there are a few 'fairy tales' from citizenship applicants, most applicants find the citizenship journey arduous, even after they have successfully overcome prolonged struggles to secure ILR or permanent settlement. Many migrant–citizens describe deeply disturbing experiences of their encounters with nationality law and procedures that are detrimental to 'feeling' British. Their stories take us beyond the usual discussions of identity and integration as, through their words, it is possible to experience their ordeals and to understand why they persisted despite significant difficulties. We can surmise from the stories that, while citizenship is profoundly meaningful to many, the processes in law to acquire citizenship are mostly meaningless to all.

The uniqueness of British citizenship

In terms of international comparisons, the British situation is unique for a number of reasons. Britain's former colonial legacy steadily morphed into the Commonwealth network of nations, which resulted in the creation of a large number of categories of potential citizenship rights holders. Disputes about who can put those rights into practice have punctuated British nationality case law and led to legislative changes in the area. The historical significance of different categories of British citizenship continues to govern the citizenship claims of many. There are many shadow areas of citizenship outside full passport-holding status. For example, a certificate of entitlement such as held by Sonia (see Chapter Four) provides the holder with the right of abode in the UK and confers freedom from UK immigration control. Over the years, the certificate has been called a partiality certificate, which then became a certificate to the right of abode, and has now become the certificate of entitlement to the right of abode, but is in essence the same document creating the very same legal entitlements.

Brexit and citizenship pathways

In the present context, Brexit plans for the UK to withdraw from the European Union (EU) have rendered EEA nationals in the UK vulnerable to immigration control in a manner unprecedented in the region. The current position taken by the Home Office is that all EU nationals and their family members will need to obtain relevant documents to confirm their status in the UK.[26] The documents will evidence that they have permission to continue living and working in the UK. This arrangement will be in place until 29 March 2019 when there will be a shift in policy depending on the arrangements that are put in place. Many long-term resident EU nationals remain uncertain of how their rights will be affected, especially in terms of acquiring British citizenship. Bernard Ryan writes in a briefing paper that some categories of person with EU free movement rights who have been resident in the United Kingdom will be left without a right to reside in the United Kingdom after Brexit.[27] It is likely that new measures will be put in place to ensure that EU nationals are treated in the same manner as other naturalising applicants. The Immigration Law Practitioner's Association (ILPA) suggests that whatever new measure comes into existence there will be a process of registration of all EEA nationals and their family members residing in the UK. ILPA's research indicates that the Home Offices does not currently have the capacity to register EEA nationals in the UK and this lack of capacity will cause hardship for EU nationals who are UK residents.[28]

The changing nature of British citizenship

Both post-Commonwealth Britain and the pre-Brexit Britain share a resurgence of limited national membership over transnational citizenship. Although concepts such as 'transnational citizenship', 'global citizenship' and 'post-national citizenship' have emerged (Falk, 1993; Bauböck, 1994; Bosniak, 2000, p 449) in both periods, British citizenship has become exclusive and exclusionary. Undergirding the uniqueness of the British situation and its exclusionary nature is the search for a basic set of 'British values' to cement British society because of its growing diversity (Tyler, 2010; Waite, 2012). Although British citizenship is of liberal make-up, it has now become a hunt for the unicorn named 'majoritarian sameness'. Although anti-racist and feminist political theorists have tried to develop alternative theories of citizenship that encompass difference, there does not seem to be any room for accounting for differences in procedures for application to citizenship.

Yet, there is no reason for British citizenship to be value-based or to be limited to an ethnic majoritarian conception. British citizenship does not have a thick civic participation requirement that is often linked to the ancient Greek city-state model of citizenship. It draws more from a minimalist, formal legal framework of citizenship such as the kind favoured by the Romans in the days of the Roman Empire. According to J. G. A. Pocock (1998), the Roman emphasis on law changed the nature of citizenship. As it became more impersonal and universal, it could embrace an empire-wide notion of citizenship. This is very much the kind of citizenship the British Empire also incorporated through the idea of subjecthood. In the Greek vision of city-state citizenship, civic participation was essential, but active citizenship has never been a specific feature of British citizenship. For acquisition of citizenship, active ingredients can only act as barriers as migrants are not able to fully participate in society until they have citizenship. There are limitations placed on their ability to move freely or work for employers until they are accepted as citizens.

As British citizenship, like the Roman variety, is based on formal equality, it can apply to diverse people more easily and without the placement of onerous duties. Formal equality need not mean treating those who are placed differently the same in law. For example, older applicants, young children and those less able to pay fees are all differently placed, and taking into consideration those differences is essential for fairness. It is true that the Roman idea of formal equality does not provide a very thick concept of citizenship, but, nevertheless, it provides legal protection of a kind valuable to most migrants. If one thinks of ILR as subsidiary citizenship, that status also provides some protection without requiring active participation from potential citizens.

Despite having potential to be a protective tool and a vehicle for fairness, British nationality law has become Kafkaesque. As a result, there is bureaucratic dehumanisation: 'The specialisation of tasks is coordinated through a circuitry of rules and regulations that appear to take the place of human action or decision making' (Ewick and Silbey, 1998, p 89) Yet, Patricia Ewick and Susan Silbey (1998, p 227) also point out that bureaucracies have productive capacity:

> ... bureaucratised procedures both enable and limit what is done and what can be done, what is possible and what is not possible. The hierarchy of offices and specialisation of tasks, characteristic of the formal bureaucracy, creates a sequence of action.

While a dehumanised, checklist approach to applications is detrimental to applicants' efforts and experiences of the application process, the process can be simplified and also made more personalised and 'human' through employing the bureaucratic capacity of immigration and nationality services. There are some attempts to make the citizenship journey more about people than processes, for example, in citizenship ceremonies. This is, however, too late and too symbolic for fostering any real sense of belonging or supporting applicants in the citizenship journey.

A few recommendations for the Home Office

Apart from developing a more fine-textured understanding of citizenship and belonging, it is possible to treat the stories in this book as a form of user feedback from successful citizenship applicants. This section offers some key suggestions for improvement. Home Office officials should consider seriously the main challenges encountered by applicants, that is, lack of fairness, lack of clarity and lack of certainty of process as well as paucity of resources. Expense is also a serious concern for most applicants. At present, the fees operate to generate revenue and commodify citizenship in an unfair and exclusionary manner. Applications should be treated at cost and, in some instances, there should be fee waivers, (for example, for children who are long-term residents but located in precarious families). The convoluted nature of citizenship applications should be simplified. There should be clarity about documentation requirements and plans to reduce paperwork. Gathering unnecessary supporting evidence is both expensive and time-consuming for applicants.

Legal advice and expertise should be available for citizenship and nationality applications. Finally, as Brexit negotiations unfold, the best way to conclude to reiterate the need for the protection of EEA long-term resident nationals in the UK. They should be provided with secure routes of entry into British citizenship, irrespective of the outcome of negotiations.

Life stories: learning from the past

The traumatic life stories of British overseas citizens and British protected persons who had no legal certainty in the UK in the 1960s–80s should not be forgotten in the process of structuring new nationality provisions for long-term resident EEA nationals in the UK. A fair nationality and immigration system based on research on life stories would contribute to a reason-based manner of operation rather than one founded on inertia or misdirected action. To quote Nobel prize-winning poet Rabindrabath Tagore:

> Where knowledge is free;… Where words come out from the depth of truth;
> Where tireless striving stretches its arms towards perfection;
> Where the clear stream of reason has not lost its way into the dreary desert sand of dead habit;…[29]

There and then, it will be possible to welcome new migrant–citizens as true equals who belong to British society.

Notes

1. Jo Cox was a Labour MP who was fatally shot and stabbed on 16 June 2016 by an attacker with Neo-Nazi links just before she was about to hold a constituency surgery. A Foundation has been set up in her memory: www.jocoxfoundation.org/ which sets out her 'more in common' quote.

2. http://archive.poetrysociety.org.uk/content/archives/places/bbcagard/remship.

3. For example, see the Kennel Club UK webpage at www.thekennelclub.org.uk/training/good-citizen-dog-training-scheme.

4. The treaty entered into force on 1 November 1993.

5. www.independent.co.uk/news/uk/politics/david-cameron-christmas-message-pm-to-hail-britains-christian-values-a6785021.html

6. www.britishpoliticalspeech.org/speech-archive.htm?speech=316

7. Mr Miller wanted to be named, so his story is not anonymised.

8. This is reminiscent of the Bourdieusian approach of connecting different fields of research (for example, Prabhat, 2016).

9. www.kent.ac.uk/law/fjp

10. www.slsa.ac.uk/images/conferences/SLSA-2017-Programme.pdf, at page 10.

11. On 18 November 2014 Scotland conducted a referendum on whether to become independent of the UK. The 'No' vote won with over 55% of the votes.

12. 'I am a migrant' stories, https://iamamigrant.org/stories?field_country_of_origin_tid_selective=All&field_current_country_tid_selective=191&field_hashtag_tid_selective=All.

13. Interview data, London-based lawyer nationality practitioner.

14. 'Immigrants in their own words – 100 stories', www.theguardian.com/commentisfree/ng-interactive/2015/mar/24/immigrants-in-their-own-words-100-stories.

15. 'I am a migrant' stories; see note 10.

[16] 'Kamila Shamsie on applying for British citizenship: "I never felt safe"', www.theguardian.com/uk-news/2014/mar/04/author-kamila-shamsie-british-citizen-indefinite-leave-to-remain.

[17] 'Home Office makes thousands in profit on some visa applications', www.theguardian.com/uk-news/2017/sep/01/home-office-makes-800-profit-on-some-visa-applications.

[18] Home Office response to freedom of information request (reference 41228) 31 October 2016, cited in 'Briefing for parliamentarians on Home Office fees for children registering as British citizens', prepared by Project for Registration of Children as British Citizens (PRCBC), https://prcbc.files.wordpress.com/2015/08/briefing-on-fees1.pdf. PRCBC recently challenged the children's registration fee and the profit making from it in the High Court, but did not succeed in getting a favourable order (*VF (litigation friend OT) v SSHD*). Full hearing on 23 November 2017.

[19] See note 14.

[20] Minimum income for British citizens to bring non-European spouses, currently set at £18,600. See www.gov.uk/uk-family-visa/proof-income and the Supreme Court case of *R (on the application of MM (Lebanon)) v Secretary of State for the Home Department* [2017] UKSC 10; 22 February 2017.

[21] Tabitha opted to waive anonymity and asked for her full name to be published.

[22] www.theguardian.com/commentisfree/ng-interactive/2015/mar/24/immigrants-in-their-own-words-100-stories.

[23] Source: 'I am a migrant' stories; see note 10.

[24] Two vans displaying the slogan 'Go home or face arrest' for undocumented migrants were driven around the country in 2013.

[25] See note 14.

[26] www.gov.uk/guidance/status-of-eu-nationals-in-the-uk-what-you-need-to-know

[27] www.ilpa.org.uk/resources.php/33749/ilpa-briefing-paper-who-will-remain-after-brexit-ensuring-protection-for-all-persons-resident-under-

[28] ILPA Briefing Paper, *Brexit 14: Status of EU Nationals in the UK following Brexit* (15 January 2018) available at: www.ilpa.org.uk/resources.php/33866/brexit-14-status-of-eu-nationals-in-the-uk-following-brexit-15-january-2018

[29] www.poets.org/poetsorg/poem/gitanjali-35

References

Abrams, P. (2007) 'We the people and other constitutional tales: teaching constitutional meaning through narrative', *The Law Teacher*, vol 4, no 3, pp 247-59.

Ackers, L. and Dwyer, P. (2004) 'Fixed laws, fluid lives: the citizenship status of post-retirement migrants in the European Union', *Ageing & Society*, vol 24, no 3, pp 451-75.

Anderson, B. (2006 [1983]) *Imagined communities* (Revised edn), London: Verso.

Anderson, B. (2010) 'Migration, immigration controls and the fashioning of precarious workers', *Work, Employment and Society*, vol 24, no 2, pp 300-17.

Anderson, B. (2013) *Us and them? The dangerous politics of immigration controls*, Oxford: Oxford University Press.

Andreouli, E. and Dashtipour, P. (2014) 'British citizenship and the "other": an analysis of the earned citizenship discourse', *Journal of Community & Applied Social Psychology*, vol 24, pp 100-10.

Antonsich, M. (2010) 'Searching for belonging – an analytical framework', *Geography Compass*, vol 4, no 6, pp 644-59.

Bascom, W. (1965) 'The forms of folklore: prose narratives', *Journal of American Folklore*, vol 78, no 307, pp 3-20.

Bauböck, R. (1994) *Transnational citizenship*, Aldershot: Edward Elgar.

Bellamy, R. (2008) 'Evaluating union citizenship: belonging, rights and participation within the EU', *Citizenship Studies*, vol 12, no 6, pp 597-611.

Benhabib, S. (2002) *The claims of culture: Equality and diversity in the global era*, Princeton, NJ: Princeton University Press.

Bhabha, J. (1999) 'Belonging in Europe: citizenship and post-national rights', *International Social Science Journal*, vol 51, no 159, pp 11-23.

Bhalla, A. and Lapeyre, F. (1997) 'Social exclusion: towards an analytical and operational framework', *Development and Change*, vol 28, no 3, pp 413-33.

Blinder, S. (2017) *Naturalisation as a British citizen: Concepts and trends*, Migration Observatory Briefing, July 2017, Oxford: COMPAS, University of Oxford, www.migrationobservatory.ox.ac.uk/resources/briefings/naturalisation-as-a-british-citizen-concepts-and-trends.

Bosniak, L. (2000) 'Universal citizenship and the problem of alienage', *Immigration and Nationality Law Review*, vol 21, pp 373-424.

Braun, V. and Clarke, V. (2006) 'Using thematic analysis in psychology', *Qualitative Research in Psychology*, vol 3, no 2, pp 77-101.

Brooks, P. and Gewirtz, P. (eds) (1998) *Laws stories: Narrative and rhetoric in the law*, New Haven, CT: Yale University Press.

Brooks, T. (2016) *Becoming British: UK citizenship examined*, London: Biteback.

Brubaker, R. (1992) *Citizenship and nationhood in France and Germany*, Cambridge, MA: Harvard University Press.

Burnett, J. (2016) *Racial violence and the Brexit state*, London: Institute of Race Relations, www.irr.org.uk/app/uploads/2016/11/Racial-violence-and-the-Brexit-state-final.pdf.

Byrne, B. (2014) *Making citizens: Public rituals and personal journeys to citizenship*, New York, NY: Palgrave Macmillan.

Carens, J.H. (2003) 'Who should get in? The ethics of immigration admissions', *Ethics & International Affairs*, vol 17, no 1, pp 95-110.

Chestek, K.D. (2012) 'Competing stories: a case study of the role of narrative reasoning in judicial decisions', *Legal Communication and Rhetoric: Journal of the Association of Legal Writing Directors*, vol 9, pp 99-137.

Cowan, D. (2004) 'Legal consciousness: some observations', *Modern Law Review*, vol 67, no 6, pp 928-58.

Crowley, J. (1999) 'The politics of belonging: some theoretical considerations', in A. Geddes and A. Favell (eds) *The politics of belonging: Migrants and minorities in contemporary Europe*, Aldershot: Ashgate, pp 15-41.

Dagger, R. (2002) 'Republican citizenship', in E.F. Isin and B.S. Turner (eds) *Handbook of citizenship studies*, London: Sage Publications, pp 145-57.

Delanty, G. (2007) 'Citizenship as a learning process: disciplinary citizenship versus cultural citizenship', Eurozine, 30 June, www.eurozine.com/citizenship-as-a-learning-process.

Delgado, R. (1989) 'Storytelling for oppositionists and others: a plea for narrative', *Michigan Law Review*, vol 87, no 8, pp 2411-41.

Dixon, J. and Durrheim, K. (2004) 'Dislocating identity: desegregation and the transformation of place', *Journal of Environmental Psychology*, vol 24, no 4, pp 455-73.

Dummett, A. and Nicol, A. (1990) *Subjects, citizens, aliens and others: Nationality and immigration law*, London: Weidenfeld & Nicolson.

Eastmond, M. (2007) 'Stories as lived experience: narratives in forced migration research', *Journal of Refugee Studies*, vol 20, no 2, pp 248-64.

Edwards, L.H. (2009) 'Once upon a time in law: myth, metaphor, and authority', *Tennessee Law Review*, vol 77, p 883.

Erel, U. (2010) 'Migrating cultural capital: Bourdieu in migration studies', *Sociology*, vol 44, no 4, pp 642-60.

Ervine, J.M. and Ervine, J. (2008) 'Citizenship and belonging in suburban France: the music of Zebda', *ACME: An International E-Journal for Critical Geographies*, vol 7, no 2, pp 199-213.

Ewick, P. and Silbey, S.S. (1998) *The common place of law: Stories from everyday life*, Chicago, IL: University of Chicago Press.

Eyster, J.P. (2008) 'Lawyer as artist: using significant moments to obtuse objects to enhance advocacy', *Legal Writing: Journal of the Legal Writing Institute*, vol 14, p 87.

Falk, R. (1993) 'The making of global citizenship', in J. Brecher, J.B. Childs and J. Cutler (eds) *Global visions: Beyond the new world order*, Boston, MA: South End, pp 39-50.

Fenster, T. (2005) 'Gender and the city: the different formations of belonging', in L. Nelson and J. Seager (eds) *A companion to feminist geography*, Malden, MA: Blackwell, pp 242-57.

Fox, J.E. and Miller-Idriss, C. (2008) 'Everyday nationhood', *Ethnicities*, vol 8, no 4, pp 536-63.

Fransman, L. (2011) *Fransman's British nationality law*, Haywards Heath: Bloomsbury Professional.

Futrell, N.S. (2015) 'Vulnerable, not voiceless: outsider narrative in advocacy against discriminatory policing', *North Carolina Law Review*, vol 93, no 5, pp 1597-639.

Getrich, C.M. (2008) 'Negotiating boundaries of social belonging: second-generation Mexican youth and the immigrant rights protests of 2006', *American Behavioral Scientist*, vol 52, no 4, pp 533-56.

Gilmartin, M. and Migge, B. (2015) 'Home stories: immigrant narratives of place and identity in contemporary Ireland', *Journal of Cultural Geography*, vol 32, no 1, pp 83-101.

Gower, M. and McGuinness, T. (2017) *Deprivation of British citizenship and withdrawal of passport facilities*, Parliamentary Briefing Paper No 06820, London: House of Commons Library.

Gray, D. and Griffin, C. (2014) 'A journey to citizenship: constructions of citizenship and identity in the British citizenship test', *British Journal of Social Psychology*, vol 53, no 2, pp 299-314.

Guild, E. (2016) *BREXIT and its consequences for UK and EU citizenship or monstrous citizenship,* Leiden/Boston, MA: Brill Nijhoff.

Habermas, J. (1992) 'Citizenship and national identity: some reflections on the future of Europe', *Praxis International*, vol 12, no 1, pp 1-19.

Habermas, J. (1994) 'Three normative models of democracy', *Constellations*, vol 1, no 1, pp 1-10.

Ho, J. (2015) *Nation and citizenship in the twentieth-century British novel*, New York, NY: Cambridge University Press.

Hunter, R., McGlynn, C. and Rackley, E. (2010) *Feminist judgments: From theory to practice*, Oxford: Hart.

Karatani, R. (2003) *Defining British citizenship: Empire, commonwealth and modern Britain*, New York, NY: Routledge.

Krieger, S.H. and Martinez, S. (2010) 'A tale of election day 2008: teaching storytelling through repeated experiences', *Legal Writing: Journal of the Legal Writing Institute*, vol 16, p 117.

Kymlicka, W. (1995) *Multicultural citizenship: A liberal theory of minority rights*, Oxford: Clarendon Press.

Kymlicka, W. and Norman, W. (1994) 'Return of the citizen: a survey of recent work on citizenship theory', *Ethics*, vol 104, no 2, pp 352-81.

Levit, N. (2009) 'Legal storytelling: the theory and the practice – reflective writing across the curriculum', *Journal of the Legal Writing Institute*, vol 15, p 259, https://ssrn.com/abstract=1144797.

Marshall, T.H. (1950) *Citizenship and social class*, Cambridge: Cambridge University Press.

May, V. (2013) *Connecting self to society: Belonging in a changing world*, Basingstoke: Palgrave Macmillan.

McNevin, A. (2006) 'Political belonging in a neoliberal era: the struggle of the sans-papiers', *Citizenship Studies*, vol 10, no 2, pp 135-51.

Mee, K. (2009) 'A space to care, a space of care: public housing, belonging, and care in inner Newcastle, Australia', *Environment and Planning A*, vol 41, no 4, pp 842-58.

Meer, N. and Modood, T. (2009) 'The multicultural state we're in: Muslims, "multiculture" and the civic re-balancing of British multiculturalism', *Political Studies*, vol 57, no 3, pp 473-97.

Meer, N., Dwyer, C. and Modood, T. (2010) 'Embodying nationhood? Conceptions of British national identity, citizenship, and gender in the "Veil Affair"', *The Sociological Review*, vol 58, no 1, pp 84-111.

Menkel-Meadow, C. (2000) 'Telling stories in school: using case studies and stories to teach legal ethics', *Fordham Law Review*, vol 69, p 787-816.

Miller, D. (1997) *On nationality*, Oxford: Clarendon Press.

Olson, G. (2014) 'Narration and narrative in legal discourse', in P. Hühn, J. Christoph Meister, J. Pier and W. Schmid (eds) *Handbook of narratology*, Berlin: De Gruyter, pp 371-83.

Pocock, J.G.A. (1998) 'The ideal of citizenship since classical times', in G. Shafir (ed) *The citizenship debates*, Minneapolis, MN: University of Minnesota, pp 31-41.

Prabhat, D. (2016) *Unleashing the force of law*, London: Palgrave.

Probyn, E. (1996) *Outside belongings*, Hove: Psychology Press.

Ryan, B.F. (2008) 'Integration requirements: a new model in migration law', *Journal of Immigration Asylum and Nationality Law*, vol 22, no 4, pp 303-16.

Ryan, L. and Mulholland, J. (2014) 'French connections: the networking strategies of French highly skilled migrants in London', *Global Networks*, vol 14, no 2, pp 148-66.

Schuck, P. (1998) *Citizens, strangers, and in-betweens*, Boulder, CO: Westview Press.

Schweitzer, R. (2015) 'A stratified right to family life? On the logic (s) and legitimacy of granting differential access to family reunification for third-country nationals living within the EU', *Journal of Ethnic and Migration Studies*, vol 41, no 13, pp 2130-48.

Shanks, L. (2007) 'Whose story is it, anyway? Guiding students to client-centered interviewing through storytelling', *Clinical Law Review*, vol 14, p 509-35.

Shilliam, R. (2016) 'Ethiopianism, Englishness, Britishness: struggles over imperial belonging', *Citizenship Studies*, vol 20, no 2, pp 243-59.

Simmel, G. (1971) 'The stranger', in D.N Levine (ed) *Georg Simmel: On individuality and social forms*, Chicago, IL: University of Chicago Press, pp 143-9.

Skey, M. (2011) *National belonging and everyday life: The significance of nationhood in an uncertain world*, Basingstoke: Palgrave Macmillan.

Stewart, E. and Mulvey, G. (2011) *Becoming British citizens?: Experiences and opinions of refugees living in Scotland*, Glasgow: Scottish Refugee Council and Strathclyde University.

Sumption, M. and Vargas-Silva, C. (2016) *The minimum income requirement for non-EEA family members in the UK*, Migration Observatory Report, June 2016, Oxford: COMPAS, University of Oxford, www.migrationobservatory.ox.ac.uk/wp-content/uploads/2016/04/Report-Minimum_Family_Income.pdf.

Turner, B.S. (2001) 'The erosion of citizenship', *British Journal of Sociology*, vol 52, no 2, pp 189-209.

Tyler, I. (2010) 'Designed to fail: a biopolitics of British citizenship,' *Citizenship Studies*, vol 14, no 1, pp 61-74.

van Oers, R. (2014) *Deserving citizenship: Citizenship tests in Germany, the Netherlands and the United Kingdom*, Leiden: Martinus Nijhoff.

van Oorschot, I. and Schinkel, W. (2015) 'The legal case file as border object: on self-reference and other-reference in criminal law', *Journal of Law and Society*, vol 42, no 4, pp 499-527.

Varsanyi, M.W. (2005) 'The rise and fall (and rise?) of non-citizen voting: immigration and the shifting scales of citizenship and suffrage in the United States', *Space & Polity*, vol 9, no 2, pp 113-34.

Waite, L. (2012) 'Neo-assimilationist citizenship and belonging policies in Britain: meanings for transnational migrants in northern England', *Geoforum*, vol 43, no 2, pp 353-61.

Waite, L. and Cook, J. (2011) 'Belonging among diasporic African communities in the UK: plurilocal homes and simultaneity of place attachments', *Emotion, Space and Society*, vol 4, no 4, pp 238-48.

Whalen-Bridge, H. (2010) 'The lost narrative: the connection between legal narrative and legal ethics', *Legal Communication and Rhetoric: Journal of the Association of Legal Writing Directors*, vol 7, pp 229-46.

Wray, H. (2011) *Regulating marriage migration into the UK: A stranger in the home*, Aldershot: Ashgate.

Wray, H. (2015) 'In family migration, men are generally regarded as economic agents and family as marginal to their lives: "a thing apart" controlling male family migration to the United Kingdom', *Men and Masculinities*, vol 18, no 4, pp 424-47.

Yuval-Davis, N. (2006) 'Belonging and the politics of belonging', *Patterns of Prejudice*, vol 40, no 3, pp 197-214.

Yuval-Davis, N. (2011) *The politics of belonging: Intersectional contestations*, London: Sage Publications.

Index